To Mummy

with love from

Jennifer + Daddy

22 Sept 1986

Jennifer
x x x

THE STORY OF
THE IMPERIAL

Gabor Denes

THE STORY OF
THE IMPERIAL

*The Life and Times of
Torquay's Great Hotel*

DAVID & CHARLES
Newton Abbot   London   North Pomfret (Vt)

British Library Cataloguing in Publication Data

Denes, Gabor
   The Imperial, Torquay.
   1. Imperial (*Hotel*)—History
   2. Hotels, taverns, etc.—England—Torquay—
History
   I. Title
   647'.94423'59501   TX941.I/
   ISBN 0-7153-8051-6

Filmset by Latimer Trend & Company Ltd, Plymouth
and printed in Great Britain
by Butler & Tanner Limited, Frome & London
for David & Charles (Publishers) Limited
Brunel House   Newton Abbot   Devon

Published in the United States of America
by David & Charles Inc
North Pomfret   Vermont 05053   USA

Contents

To Michael Chapman—Hotelier Imperial—
and his dear wife Tim

Acknowledgements

It would have been impossible to write this book without the willing and generous help received from a large number of kind people. This is to convey my grateful thanks to them all.

The unstinting assistance given by two friends stands out: John Wollen and Michael Chapman, whose personal recollections span several decades. John's go back to the mid-1920s and Michael's to the beginning of the last war—I cannot thank them enough.

Others who have provided essential information, or the means for gaining it, include the following (in alphabetical order): Peter Bottrill (Area Librarian), Rudy Boyden, Mrs Pat Bray (*Herald Express*), Michael Dowdell (Central Library, Torquay), Dennis Eldergill, Roy Hayter (Inf Officer, HCIMA), Dr W. Holden and K. Leach (and all the staff at the Torquay Natural History Society's Museum), R. Lang, Mrs P. Kitley-Carter, Billy Munn, Harry Murray, Miss Joyce Packe, Miss L. D. Randall, Leslie Retallick (Torre Abbey), T. Russell (Secretary, THF Hotels Ltd), R. J. D. Smith (*Herald Express*), Mike Sangster, W. Scobie, Stanley G. Straw, John Baker White and Nigel Wollen.

Finally, last but by no means least, I want to express my infinite gratitude to my dear wife, not only for her indefatigable collaboration in my research, but also for all the moral support and encouragement she has given me during the birth of this book.

G.D.

Author's Introduction

To start this story at the beginning would mean going back about 120 years, to the early part of Queen Victoria's reign. However, instead of plunging straight away into those far away times, I would like to explain, briefly, how and why the story came to be written. This involves not more than a quarter of a century of backtracking in time . . . to mid-summer 1956, to be exact.

That was the time of my first visit to the subject of my story, and I have never forgotten the impact of that first encounter, which took place under ideal conditions. Being very much involved at that time in writing on nautical subjects, especially sailing, I went to Torquay to cover a unique event for some specialist and glossy magazines: the start of the first ever international Sail Training Ship Race.

I made my headquarters during those few days leading up to the actual start on 7 July at The Imperial, which of course was the perfect spot to be in; not only was it the centre of many of the social events attended by the top people involved in the race—admirals, ambassadors and world-famous sailing personalities—but it offered the miraculous view of the last few great sailing ships in that perfect and unique setting of the blue waters of Torbay.

I greatly enjoyed it all, the receptions held in delightful surroundings, the gardens on the waterside of the Royal Dart YC, on board the Portuguese barque *Sagres*, the staysail schooner *Creole*, owned by Stavros Niarchos, at Oldway Mansions, Paignton and finally, on the eve of the start of the race, a huge reception and a small dinner party given by the organisers at The Imperial itself.

Those few days at the hotel were extremely pleasant. Having stayed in some of the world's greatest hotels during my years of travel, I could not fail to recognise and appreciate the inherent qualities and atmosphere of the place, and looking back to the experience from a safe distance of decades, I feel sure that my feelings must have been akin to falling in love. It was certainly the beginning of a relationship much more enduring than most human ones. For it has lasted, and is still going strong.

9

On that first visit I was befriended by the charming and dynamic Managing Director, Michael Chapman (there will be much more about him in the later chapters of this book), who appeared to be well aware of the importance of promoting the image of his hotel to a wider audience. The outcome of our conversations was my appointment as public relations consultant. I had already made up my mind and have always been fortunate to maintain that I would only take on work that I could enjoy. This has proved to be the case over the last twenty-five years; my work for The Imperial has been invariably interesting, challenging and most enjoyable. It has also enabled me to make a large number of friends among the staff—from the Managing Director to the valets and waiters.

An amusing small sidelight comes to my mind, in the shape of a remark made years later by one of the long-serving waiters in the restaurant, called Taffy. Whenever I was there we always had a little friendly conversation. On this occasion he said: 'It's a long time since you first came here Mr Denes . . . I remember well when you first arrived—you came ashore from that lovely sailing ship the *Creole.*' This made me feel like some long-forgotten Greek god having emerged from the waves.

Over the years my interest in The Imperial grew apace, and it was only natural that I should become intrigued with its history, right from the conception of the idea. A certain amount of information on the early beginnings emerged when we celebrated the hundredth anniversary of the opening in 1966. Stimulated by the few details I started looking for more facts relating to the hotel's beginnings, early life and development. These were not always easy to come by, but little by little it became possible to put the fragments from various surviving sources together and turn them into one coherent and fascinating story.

To call my story fascinating is not an idle exaggeration. I feel that the story of The Imperial is not only the greatly edifying account of a fine example of outstanding achievement in a very difficult field of human endeavour and enterprise. It is more than that; it also brings to light many facets of the life of our not so distant forebears, their way of life and ever-changing attitudes to life.

Enchantment has been my reward frequently while turning the pages of forgotten annals—figuratively speaking—and it is my sincere hope that I have succeeded in conveying at least some of the delights to my readers. After this attempt at explaining my reasons and reactions, it is time we got on to the chronological beginning . . .

1
In The Beginning

1

By the middle of the nineteenth century, Torquay was well on the way to becoming recognised as a desirable resort town. Its fundamental attraction had arisen from its fortunate geographical situation on the shore of Torbay. Through centuries of war and peace—more war than peace—before the end of the sailing-ship era, this magnificent bay, its waters protected from all but the due south-easterly winds, has been a much favoured sheltered anchorage and has gained an honourable place in England's naval history.

Charles Kingsley referred to one of the early episodes:

> We cannot gaze on its blue ring of water, and the great limestone bluffs which bound it to the north and south, without a glow passing through our hearts, as we remember the terrible and glorious pageant which passed by in the glorious July days of 1588, when the Spanish Armada ventured slowly past Berry Head with Elizabeth's gallant pack of Devon captains (for the London fleet had not yet joined) following fast in its wake, and dashing into the midst of the vast line, undismayed by size and numbers, while their kin and friends stood watching and praying on the cliffs, spectators of Britain's Salamis.

Almost exactly a hundred years later, in November 1688, William of Orange changed the course of English history when he sailed into Torbay leading his fleet of warships from Holland, carrying 15,000 men and landed at Brixham. During the next century, when England was at war with France for nearly six decades, the Torbay anchorage sheltered the English Channel Fleet between its frequent sorties in pursuit of the enemy, such as the blockade of Brest and the battle of Quiberon Bay.

Napoleon Bonaparte, after his return from Elba and his Hundred Days' adventure ended by Waterloo, was brought from France to Torbay as a prisoner on board the *Bellerophon* in July 1815. His presence created enormous interest, and during the weeks that followed the ship was constantly surrounded by boats and yachts carrying curious spectators hoping to catch a glimpse of the Emperor. 'Torbay presented just such an animated appearance as is often witnessed on a regatta day' wrote a chronicler of the day. When he first saw the scenery of Torbay, Napoleon is said to have exclaimed: '*Enfin voila ce beau pays!*' to which he added the further comment: 'It is like Porto Ferrajo in Elba.' Quite a compliment this, for one would not expect Napoleon, or any Frenchman in his position, to flatter the English.

From a quiet, insignificant village, Torquay began to develop into a thriving, fashionable town during the first quarter of the nineteenth century. Growth was stimulated by the actions of the big landowners, prominent among them being the two leading families, the Carys and the Palks, who granted leases for the building of suitable residences for the growing population.

It has been often thought that Torquay owed its early rise to the Navy's presence in the Bay; it has been claimed that development was due to the demand for residential accommodation for naval officers' families during the Napoleonic wars. This is firmly contradicted by the opposing view, which holds that Torquay became desirable purely on account of its remarkable climate. An early reference to the resort's development is found in the *Guide to the Watering Places of South Devon* (1817) stating bluntly that the new town of Torquay 'was built to accommodate invalids'. A later publication, *Panorama of Torquay* (1832) states:

> ... the salubrious climate of Torquay appears to have attracted attention; and it is, we believe, from that period that we must date its rise and progress. When therefore subsequent observations had confirmed the testimony of public opinion in its favour, houses were erected for the accommodation of the invalids, who annually migrate from the colder parts of the Island to Devonshire ... The surroundings give it a superiority over other watering places on the coast, and induce many families to select it as a permanent residence.

The writer of the above, Octavian Blewitt, went on quoting Dr Clark, a noted physician of the day, showing that the average temperature was markedly higher than other favoured resorts, such as Cheltenham or Sidmouth. 'For those with consumptive tendencies, Torquay was the finest possible place to be in, sheltered from every cold wind and offering an almost 'Italian' air. If one favoured a higher elevation than the harbourside terraces, the villas on the slopes of the hills afforded it. To those who thought it relaxing in summer, the answer was that the vales of Upton and of Chelston, the avenues of the Abbey were always refreshing ...'

The growth of the town, resplendent with much attractive Regency and early Victorian architecture, was further stimulated by

Torquay, view from the pier, about 1835

the coming of the railway. The main line from Bristol and Exeter had already been extended to Newton Abbot and opened at the end of 1846. Before this the traffic between Exeter and Torquay was maintained by mail coaches which had their terminus at the Royal Hotel, doubtless the leading establishment at the time. The journey via Teignmouth took four hours, and the other service, the *Victoria*, travelling through Newton and Chudleigh, took about the same time; they also ran to Dartmouth and another one to Plymouth.

The first extension of the railway from Newton Abbot was completed—after a great deal of argument and haggling over land—as far as Torre and opened with due ceremony and widespread celebration on 15 December 1848. This did not satisfy everyone, however, and further years of wrangling followed. Torquay's inhabitants did not want to have the railway cross the town right down to the harbour, the then powerful fishing interests of Brixham needed the railway to serve their needs, and finally the solution emerged: Torquay station at Livermead, and the line continuing to Paignton towards Dartmouth. The first train arrived at Torquay station on 11 July 1859.

Torquay had been discovered as a seaside and health resort, but around the middle of the nineteenth century the facilities for visitors were still far from copious. Around 1850–60 there were a few hotels, but the total number of their rooms did not add up to much more than

150; about 70 small lodging or boarding houses probably brought the total number of rooms in the town available to visitors to around 500.

Hitherto the developers and what today would be called the planners (I don't suppose the expression had been invented) relied on the well-to-do winter and spring visitors, who for the most part rented whole houses for the season for themselves and their numerous servants. As late as 1871 there were thousands more females than males among the local population so there was always an ample supply of domestic servants. Villas proliferated during the first half of the century, and the evidence of the fashionable status acquired by Torquay is in the number of high-ranking and illustrious people who regularly made their escape from the rigours of winter to Torquay. Dowager Queen Adelaide was at Apsley House in 1845, ex-Queen Marie of France in 1854. In the same year Charles Kingsley was at Livermead House; Bulwer Lord Lytton bought Argyll Hall (now a hotel under another name) in 1856, to live and work there for nearly twenty years; Baroness Burdett Coutts, the great benefactress of the Church of England, lived at Ehrenberg Hall for fifteen years.

By 1863 it was clear to one of the leading planners of the town and his associates that the time was ripe for something more ambitious: a hotel of high quality, fit for the highest in the land. Only such an establishment would raise Torquay to the level of the best winter resorts, including the highly desirable and fashionable ones in the South of France . . .

2

Early Days

2

It was at the initiative of Sir Lawrence Palk, Bart, MP, that the Torquay Hotel Company was formed, and the first meeting of its directors was held under his chairmanship on 1 July 1863. The company was registered under the recent Limited Liability Act of 1862—the registration certificate which survives has the serial number 500.

The next meeting of the directors was held less than a fortnight later, and not to lose too much time, it was resolved to purchase the leases of two villas, the Cove and the Cliff, their site offering the most suitable clifftop position for the new venture. A new lease of the site was to be granted by the landowner (Sir Lawrence Palk, Bart, MP, who else?) for 99 years. The ground rent amounted to all of £60 per annum.

The declared purpose of the new company, formed with a total share capital of £70,000, was to acquire the existing Royal Hotel with its stables and to build a new, larger hotel, to be bigger and better than

Webb's Royal Hotel, about 1852

any other existing in Torquay. Plans were prepared by the architect, E. N. Clifton, to the instructions of the directors, which stipulated 'a building upon the site purchased by the Company showing the extent to which an Hotel could be built for £40,000, and also what portion might be taken from it so as to make the expenditure £25,000'. The plans were approved and tenders from builders were invited in a number of newspapers, including *The Times*, the *Observer*, and several regional and local as well as building trade papers.

Progress must have been quick and smooth, for in February 1864 Mr Clifton, the architect, was asked 'to make arrangements to lay the foundation stone of the new hotel on Easter Monday'. Two directors, Messrs Wells and Cholmondley, were delegated to 'wait upon Lady Palk and request her to lay the foundation stone ...' At the same meeting it was resolved that 'a sum not exceeding £12 be expended upon a trowel'. It must have been a good-quality trowel, if we consider that about the same time the board agreed that the auditor of the company should be paid two guineas (£2.10) per audit.

On Easter Monday, 28 March 1864, the foundation stone was duly and ceremoniously laid; it enclosed a parchment with the following inscription:

> The foundation stone of the Torquay Hotel Company was laid on Monday, the 28th of March 1864, by Maria Harriet, wife of Sir Lawrence Vaughan Palk, Bart., M.P. of the county of Devon.
> Directors, Sir L. Palk, Bart, Chairman; Edw. Gulson, Deputy-Chairman; Lord Allan Spencer Churchill, C. G. Cholmondley Esq., Lawson Cape Esq., W. F. Splatt Esq., I. B. Toogood Esq., W. Robertson Esq., G. E. Wells Esq., N. F. Uniacke Esq., Sec.
> Architect E. N. Clifton Esq.; Solicitor W. Toogood Esq.; Contractor, Mr. Drake; Auditor Mr. John Kitson.

At the ceremony, which was attended by the directors, shareholders 'and other members of the nobility', it was the Deputy Chairman who made the formal request to the lady to perform, 'in a graceful address'. 'Lady Palk spread the mortar, and the massive stone was laid in its place.' Mr Gulson thanked her profusely in yet another address, reported in full by the press. He included this fulsome tribute: 'If anything can enhance the charms which you have deigned to throw over our proceedings by your co-operation this day, it is the beauty of the spot on which we are assembled, and in which the new hotel is to be erected. And if, as the building proceeds to its completion it should prove worthy of your patronage and approval, and of the kind exertions you have this day made on our behalf, the numerous and

distinguished visitors of Torquay will be provided with accommodation, unrivalled in climate, beauty of situation, and comfort, by
any in the Kingdom. And an element of attraction for their beautiful
locality; and if the management should fortunately be such as we hope
to secure, the shareholders no doubt will have equal reason to be
satisfied with the result of the undertaking . . .'

The aims, hopes and ambitions of the directors are also reflected in
the brief speech with which Sir Lawrence himself brought the
proceedings to a close. To quote an even briefer extract: '. . . we shall
carry with us the success that has already crowned the undertaking; and
while we give that accommodation to the public which is so much
required, we shall be able to earn for the shareholders a fair return for
the money they have invested . . . The advantages of this situation few
other places can show; it is unrivalled in the West of England; and I
believe there is no place in the town of Torquay where the climate is so
mild, or the scenery more beautiful. I cannot for a moment doubt that
under such favourable auspices our undertaking will meet with
success, and in a very short time we shall have the pleasure of calling
our friends again together to celebrate the completion of that which we
have begun today.'

It will be noted that, strangely, during all these celebrations the
great hotel of the future remained nameless; throughout, it was spoken
of simply as 'the hotel' or 'the new hotel'. There is no indication
anywhere in the records that the question was raised by anyone
concerned. One wonders if there might have been a person who,
perhaps out of simple curiosity, raised the question at the stone-laying
ceremony: 'I wonder what this wonderful new hotel is to be called?' If
there was such an inquisitive soul, we may rest assured they got no
answer. We shall have it a little later.

THE YEARS OF PREPARATION

Times have changed a great deal in well over a hundred years, but the
trials, tribulations, problems and delays that faced the owners of the
emerging hotel are not all that different from those that would be
experienced in the progress of a similar enterprise today. We have no
complete record of the years between the laying of the foundation
stone and the opening; most of the information gleaned is from the
minutes of directors' meetings, providing only fragmentary evidence of
what was going on.

There must have been some trouble between the company and the building contractors; it was clearly a case of changing horses midstream, for there appears to have been a court case brought against the company by the original contractor, a Mr Drake, and a trial took place at Bristol. In August 1864 the seal of the company was fixed to the contract with the new builder, Mr Matcham. In January 1865 a new secretary to the company was appointed at the princely honorarium of £50 per annum.

During the early part of 1865 the directors showed the first signs of becoming somewhat restless concerning the slow progress of the work at the site, and in February the meeting resolved 'that a letter to be written to Mr. Clifton [the architect], asking him to send a report to the directors of the state of the new buildings, to state how soon he could get the roof on, and informing him that the directors were in hopes that further progress would have been made before then.' At the same time Mr Clifton was to be asked if it was time for inviting tenders for the heating of the premises and for the necessary ranges, and also 'whether anything could be done towards forming terraces.' For the next meeting the estimates for the additional work were submitted and duly authorised by the board. At the same time the building was insured in the vast sum of £1,000!

In July 1865 the directors found it necessary again to send a letter to Mr Clifton expressing their 'surprise and dissatisfaction that no further progress had been made in the new Hotel' . . . All these delays must have had their effect on the growing costs, for three months later it was resolved that debentures be issued to the tune of £20,000. The directors must have become more and more exasperated, for by the end of March 1866 they demanded a straight undertaking from the architect as to when—in his opinion—the building would be handed over by the contractor. At the same time, Mr Thomas Webb (previously manager of the Royal Hotel and then a member of the board) was asked to draw up a list of 'articles' required for furnishing the new hotel.

Progress was made in slow stages. At last the directors got down to brass tacks—they decided to get rid of the silver plate (Sheffield) and to purchase the more up-to-date electro-plate instead. Things were really moving now; early in May 1866 they accepted the offer from a reputable firm to supply all the carpet needed for the hotel; it was to be 'five thread Brussels best quality, be laid and fixed by the 20th July then next for the sum of 5/6d [27½ pence] per yard'. At about the same time it appeared to the directors that 'for the purpose of completing and furnishing the new hotel the sum of £8,000 was necessary to be raised in addition to the sums already raised by debentures, and that a proposition to be made to the Chairman of the company (Sir Lawrence Palk, Bart, MP) that if he would undertake to raise the sum of £4,000, the other directors would raise the remaining £4,000.'

An even more momentous decision was made on the same day (22 May 1866): to name the new venture *The Imperial Hotel*; this could not be delayed much longer with the opening only a few months away, and it was a felicitous choice, something for the future hotel to live up to. Time was pressing and early in July 1866 Thomas Webb was appointed the first Manager of the new Imperial Hotel, 'for the term of five to seven years at a salary equivalent to one-fourth part of all net profits realised'. About a month before the opening the amount of 'insurance on the building' was increased to £18,000.

There is a reliable record of the formal opening in the following extract from the *Torquay Times and South Devon Advertiser*:

Saturday, November 3rd, 1866:

THE IMPERIAL, TORQUAY

The colossal structure of which our readers have heard so much and taken an admiring view, designated most appropriately the 'Imperial' Hotel, is now opened for the reception of the 'distingues' who in the season crowd to Torquay.

It is grand, magnificent, imposing, delightfully situated on one of the most charming spots of the picturesque shore of Torbay, completely sheltered from cold winds, commanding an unrivalled view of land and sea, surrounded by ornamental gardens in which visitors may freely breathe the far-famed air of the district, abounding with every luxury and convenience, arranged for the comfort of guests, close to the baths and the principal parts of the town, what more could be desired in the best hotel that was ever built.

As will be seen from the arrival list the 'fashionable' have not been tardy in their patronage of the establishment. To inaugurate the opening, a select party of the directors and friends sat down to a sumptuous dinner à la Russe. Every one of the delicacies of the season was duly represented on the table which presented a most magnificent appearance. The boudoir had been handsomely decorated, perfumed and fitted up for the occasion.

Among those present were Sir L. Palk Bt, M.P. and Lady Palk, Col. Campbell (of Possit) and Mrs Campbell, Mr & Mrs J. B. Toogood, Mr & Mrs C. Kitson, Mr & Mrs W. H. Kitson, Capt & Mrs Mullins, etc. etc.

Round's Band was in attendance and played a choice selection of music. At the conclusion of the repast dancing in the coffee room was begun and a card party was also made up. The greatest gratification at the arrangements was expressed by the guests.

The Imperial Hotel was opened in 1866

The following description was inspired if not written in its total by Thomas Webb, the Manager, and issued to prospective clients in the period immediately following the opening:

THE IMPERIAL HOTEL, TORQUAY

The Hotel is built in the Italian style of architecture which harmonises with the rich scenery around.

No expense has been spared in providing in this hotel the Comforts and Elegance of Life to which our patrons are accustomed, as can be imagined when it is learned that the cost of the building alone was between £30,000 and £40,000, and almost as much again was spent on the accoutrements.

On the sea, or south, side of the basement a Terrace Walk, laid with coloured tiles, runs the whole length of the building. On the ground floor there is a beautiful arcade of the same length, resting on ornamental pillars and arches. On the first floor there is a massive Portland stone balcony along the whole extent of the sea frontage, and on the second floor there are large lead flats to every bay window, enclosed with balustrades. All the windows have decorated zinc verandahs and shades.

The interior

The Main Entrance is on the north side, and is reached by a capacious Carriage Drive. The Doorway is protected by a Portico of noble proportions and architectural beauty. Your carriage can drive beneath it and set down its passenger at the door with no inconvenience from inclement weather.

The Vestibule is enclosed Spanish mahogany fittings and embossed glass, and on the left there is a telegraph office and the clerk's room.

The Hall, the broad and handsome Grand Staircase, and the Corridor are very splendid. The floors are laid with encaustic tiles in beautiful designs. Sienna marble pilasters with enriched capitals decorate the corridor, which is one hundred feet long, seventeen feet broad and nineteen feet high. It has Italian marble skirtings and arches which are highly ornamental, being picked out in harmonious colours. Doors on either side lead to Drawing- and Bed-rooms, those on the south side having delightful views across the waters of Tor Bay.

At the south-western corner is the Gentlemen's Coffee Room, most luxuriously furnished, with brackets and chandeliers of Florentine bronze of elegant design. The attendance of servants is obtained by touching a handle, which strikes a gong outside. Nearby is a lavatory supplied with hot and cold water, and next to this is a Ladies' Coffee Room, which has a Brazilian marble mantelpiece.

In the same part of the building is the second-best staircase of solid Portland stone. At various parts of the hall and corridor are placed marble pedestals with statues. The elegant corridor on the first floor is enclosed in circular roof of embossed plate glass of a beautiful and chaste pattern.

On this floor the rooms are arranged in Suites, the door of the lobby closing the suite to the corridor in the same manner as a street door, so that the suite has the privacy of a distinct house. There are bath rooms on this floor. In the chambermaid's room there is a congerie of bells, so that your domestics may easily be summoned when you require their attendance, and in various places there are speaking tubes by which communication may be made with the basement storey.

The basement storey is fireproof. The kitchen is admirably fitted up and, as is the cuisine, is thought to be the best outside London. It has a range, the spits being turned by a mechanical contrivance that is set in motion by a draught in the chimney. There are two fires commanding three ovens; a grilling stove, and a panmarie heated by steam and three hot closets in which dinners can be kept warm by steam. The kitchen too is fitted with speaking tubes for communicating with servants' rooms, to ensure prompt service when meals are awaited.

For the convenience of those who do not wish to bring their own carriages, flys and omnibuses meet all principal trains at the railway station to convey patrons to the Imperial Hotel.

During the first week in which it was open, the Imperial Hotel enjoyed the patronage of the following ladies and gentlemen, who kindly expressed their appreciation of the arrangements of the hotel, which satisfy the requirements of the most fastidious: The Lady Codrington and family; The Hon. Lady Abercrombie and family; Sir Lawrence Palk Bart. and Lady Palk; Mr and Mrs C. F. Malcolmson; Mr and Mrs Scriven; Mr and Mrs Price; Mrs May and family; Mr and Mrs Clifton; Mr and Mrs Laverton; Mr and Mrs Dunn; Captain Cutler R.N.; Mr M. Bentley and Mr D'Arcy.

If you favour the hotel with your esteemed custom, the Manager respectfully assures you of his best attention at all times.

THOMAS WEBB
Manager.

In January 1867 the following advertisement appeared repeatedly in *The Torquay Directory* (a weekly newspaper, founded 1840):

THE IMPERIAL HOTEL

Mr Thomas Webb begs respectfully to inform the public generally that the above Hotel which is replete with every improvement for the comfort of visitors is NOW OPENED.

The Rooms are arranged en suite with a Ladies Coffee Room, Reading Room etc. The Situation is unrivalled, facing and near the Sea with South aspect, near the Club, the Baths, the Beacon Hill and the Post Office.

OPEN and CLOSED CARRIAGES, POST HORSES etc. Omnibuses and Flys belonging to the Hotel meet the trains.

View from the Beacon in 1866—to the left of The Imperial Hotel is seen the Villa Marina, later to become the West Wing

Success must have been instantaneous, for within less than two years of the opening the directors decided that it was 'advisable to build an additional wing of bedrooms, a Table d'Hote Room and a Smoking Room', and by 1870 it was decided to go ahead with plans prepared for this purpose.

There were other signs of the hotel prospering. It was a custom to publish the list of people staying in the three or four leading hotels every week in *The Torquay Directory*. These show excellent support, listing distinguished names, with families (and servants in some cases). Two other interesting facts emerge from these lists: the majority of guests stayed on week after week, having come for two or three months or the whole winter season. It is also clear evidence of the season being the winter in those years: the lists begin to diminish by about Easter and start growing again in October–November. In fact the winter continued to be the main season until well into the 1920s. In the early years of the hotel it appears that there was rivalry between Torquay and the French Riviera. Weather conditions were frequently compared and showed a distinct advantage in favour of Torquay. As reported in *The Torquay Directory* on 22 January 1868, the mean temperature during the preceding month of December 1867 was 39·7° at Cannes against 42·1° at Torquay, snow fell three times in Cannes and not at all in Torquay.

In the first few years after it was opened, the hotel only let about fifty bedrooms, and not surprisingly the demand for them was exceeding the supply right from the start. The fame of The Imperial Hotel spread far and wide. My old friend and neighbour, the distinguished writer, landowner and former Member of Parliament, John Baker White, has a letter in his possession, written by his paternal grandmother on 27 October 1868, while on her honeymoon, to her brother, referring to it: 'This is an awfully jolly place and very pretty, the nicest place we have been to yet!'

Royal visitors did not take long to discover the best place to patronise in beautiful Torquay. The Queen of Holland spent some weeks at the hotel on her second visit to the town (the first time she had stayed at the old Royal Hotel), arriving in February 1870. Of this visit, in fact, we have more than hearsay evidence, for inscribed on the first page of the hotel's only surviving visitors' book, covering the years 1870–78, we see in perfect copperplate handwriting the testimony of her arrival: '*Sa Majesté la Reine des Pays Bas*', followed by the full names of her entourage: '*. . . première dame d'honneur . . ., dame d'honneur*' and the names of not one but two gentlemen described as '*Chambellan de S.M.*'

The next important royal visitor unfortunately was not asked (or perhaps did not want) to sign the visitors' book, but his visit created a great deal more of a stir among the population. In September 1871, the ex-Emperor Napoleon III was recommended by his doctors to go and stay for a while at Torquay for the benefit of his health. J. T. White in his *History of Torquay* tells some of the story: 'The date of His Majesty's journey, the 11th, seems to have been well known, for at most of the railway stations on the route the people assembled and gave him a cordial greeting. At Exeter the crowds on the platform were somewhat too demonstrative. In order to avoid a crush the Torquay Station was kept clear, only a limited number of persons being admitted; but the station yard, the Torbay Road and the approaches to the Imperial Hotel, where apartments had been taken for his Majesty, the Prince Imperial, and suite, were lined with people. Sir L. Palk and Mr L. H. Palk were at the station to receive the august party. . . The Emperor was greeted with shouts of *Vive l'Empereur*! . . . Along the whole line of the route the Emperor received an ovation . . . During their stay the Emperor and the Prince Imperial took out-door exercise daily, on most occasions unattended, and they were everywhere received with demonstrations of respect.'

From other sources we learn that the Emperor and his party—the Prince Imperial, Prince Murat, le Comte Clary, M. Conneau Fils and three other friends—got up early in the mornings and after breakfast set out on walks. They liked luncheon to be served at 11 o'clock (!) and in the afternoons they went on longer walks or took a drive to the countryside, to Brixham, Totnes, Dartmouth, Plymouth or Haldon. They also enjoyed sailing and fishing expeditions in Torbay. His Majesty frequently expressed his surprise and delight at the beauty of the environment.

He was also clearly pleased with the hotel and expressed his satisfaction to the manager more than once with the service and attention received. Rather more remarkable, he particularly appreciated the cooking. After a specially enjoyable dinner during his stay he sent for the chef to congratulate him on his skill, adding that he had not enjoyed his food anywhere as much since he left France. The pleasure of both men was complete when the chef explained that up to two years ago he had been employed as a cook in the Palace of the Tuileries.

A charming incident took place during the ex-Emperor's stay, when one evening the First Company of the Torquay Rifle Volunteers marched to the carriage drive of the hotel where their band played the

French song 'Partant pour la Syrie' and 'God Save the Queen'. Napoleon III and the Prince came to the entrance portico to listen, asked for more music to be played, inspected the unit of soldiers and finally the Emperor gave a speech of thanks to the men. Before leaving Torquay, the distinguished visitor once more expressed his thanks personally to Thomas Webb, the Manager, adding that the five weeks spent at the hotel had resulted in a great improvement in his health.

By now readers must be wondering why—apart from the small incident when Napoleon III sent for the chef to congratulate him—there has been no mention of an aspect of hotel life, which in our day, over a hundred years later, would be considered most important: food and cooking. This is not due to an oversight on my part, but simply to the fact that food is almost never mentioned in the contemporary records.

There can be only one explanation, the mores and manners of the era. We know now that our Victorian forebears regarded it highly improper, and decidedly poor taste, to discuss such a mundane subject as food and drink. They must have regarded it simply as just another function of the body one does not talk about. This strange, almost hypocritical attitude seems to have extended to the discussions of the directors' meetings and the writers of books and newspapers. *Tempora mutantur...*

My own impression, based partly on the very scanty information found and partly on conjecture, would be that especially in the earliest years of this story, ie at the opening and just after, the type of food served in the best of English hotels was of a very simple, plain type. The only factual evidence is a battered, faded original menu, which came to hand during my searches; it is just possible to read the handwriting and I quote it overleaf in its entirety, spelling mistakes and all.

Looking at this menu it becomes obvious that in those early days, in any case, there could not have been much demand for 'gourmet' cooking, and also that the man (or woman?) responsible must have been a homely British person, a 'good, plain cook' only vaguely and remotely influenced by French cuisine.

It was not long, however, before there was a radical change. It seems reasonable to suppose that the chef congratulated by Napoleon III was a Frenchman. The full impact of his arrival on the scene can best be illustrated by another menu, served at a wedding luncheon in the hotel. We read in the 23 August 1871 issue of *The Torquay Directory*:

The Imperial Hotel, Torquay

* * *

Monday 25 March 1867

* * *

Table d'Hote.

* * *

BILL OF FARE

* * *

SOUPS

Mulligatawny

Shrimp

Oyster

* * *

FISH

Turbot & Lobster Sauce

Salmon

Fried Skate

Gurnet

* * *

ENTREES

Rissoles de Homard

Riz de Veau à l'Italienne

Poulet à la Meringo

Cotelette de Agneau aux Petit Pois

* * *

JOINTS

Saddle Mutton

Braised Beef a la Jardinere

Fore Quarter Lamb

Boiled Fowls

Tongue

Ducks

* * *

ENTREMETS

Poudin de Cabinet

Poudin St. Clair

Junket

Gellée au Pistache

Ices

* * *

DESSERT

'There were forty guests at the fashionable wedding at St. Mary Church followed by a party, which arrived at the Imperial Hotel in eight carriages and pairs. It was the marriage of Miss Caroline O'Fallow Pope, eldest daughter of Mrs. Pope of Dartmouth to Mr Francis B. Vaughan, third son of Col. Vaughan of Herefordshire. They were married by Dr Vaughan Roman Catholic Bishop of Plymouth, uncle of the bridegroom. A magnificent dejeuner was prepared, such a sight had never been seen in Torquay before.'

Here is the whole delightful menu, as published:

SERVICE A LA RUSSE

* * *

ENTRÉES CHAUDES

Bouchées à la Reine

Filets de Boeuf à la Parisienne

* * *

RELEVES

Paté de Grouse à la Gelée

Gelatine de Poularde à la Vallière

* * *

ENTREES FROIDES

Mayonnaise de Homard au Bordure

Filets de Volaille à l'Ecarlate

Aspics de Crevettes

Salade à la Russe

Cotelettes d'Agneau au Belle Vue

* * *

GROSSES PIECES D'ENTREMETS

Biscuits à la Vanille

Grosses Meringues

* * *

ENTREMETS

Bavarois aux Avelines

Pain d'Ananas à la Gelée

Petits Gateaux Moka

* * *

DESSERTS

Deux Glaces

31

The change of style is clearly evident and we must assume that the unnamed French chef had set the tone and standard of the Imperial's kitchens for ever after. There is just another small indication of what went on in those kitchens seen in an advertisement appearing regularly at about the same period, which offers 'Invalid clear and thick turtle soup now ready and can be forwarded to any part of the Kingdom. Orders to be addressed to the Manager.' It must have been a versatile kitchen indeed.

3

The End of an Era

3

The new wing was opened in time for the autumn and winter season of 1871; it contained a new dining-room ('Table d'Hote Room') and an additional forty bedrooms. By modern standards the dining-room would not have been regarded as large, being only 70 by 35ft, but it became a sumptuous addition praised and enjoyed by the guests. The expenditure on the new wing proved well worth while, the additional bedrooms were filled without difficulty and the directors were happy. So they should have been; the total building costs amounted to all of £8,000.

Success was reflected in the year's accounts presented to the company's Annual General Meeting on 5 June 1872. The figures underlined the wisdom of the expansion, for in spite of increases in the running costs, the gross annual receipts were up to nearly £18,000, showing an increase over the previous year of almost £2,500. Correspondingly, the net profit declared came to £4,512, an imposing amount at the time, making the dividend for the shareholders an impressive 7 per cent. At the same time some new shares were offered, and were taken up without difficulty.

The visitor's book already referred to provides clear-cut evidence of the hotel's standing in the world during the 1870s. Not only members of the British nobility, but frequently leading aristocrats from the Continent were among the names found. For a typical sample of these we find the names of Prince Esterhazy of 'Pesth' (at that time Buda and Pesth had not been united to become the Hungarian capital) and of Adalbert Prince of Prussia, mingling with those of the Duchess of Sutherland, Lord Justice Mellish, the Princes John and Francis Liechtenstein of Austria, several members of the old Tsarist aristocracy, led by Alexandre Baschmakow, who was described as the Master of the Court of His Imperial Majesty the Emperor of Russia, St Petersburg, the Count and Countess Luetzow (Austria), the Master of the Rolls and Lady Jessel.

Not only the names are revealing; so are the addresses, among which we frequently read — Manor, — House, from all parts of the British

Isles, the names of many rectories and vicarages, of the great colleges of Oxford and Cambridge, the leading gentlemen's clubs in London . . . it was only members of the 'elite' who travelled and spent long holidays in luxury hotels. Several guests gave as their addresses the names of yachts belonging to members of the Royal Yacht Squadron. Some cricket elevens checked in year after year; they must have been the 'gentlemen' rather than the 'players'.

Many well-to-do people travelled for pleasure; they had not only the money but also the leisure to do so. They came from all corners of the globe, and it is surprising to find that the proportion of guests from America was so high in the years after 1870; in fact it seems to have been higher than it is in our day. Although many of them simply gave their addresses as USA, most of the others were from New York, not quite as many from Boston and fewer from Chicago, Philadelphia and other cities of the eastern States. Apart from the fact that the globe-trotting habit was beginning among successful Americans, the explanation could be that some of the best transatlantic liners put into Plymouth, no distance at all from Torquay. There were a few visitors from the far-flung outposts of the British Empire too; on one page I spotted addresses in Mauritius, Bengal, Quebec, Australia (sic), probably Britishers who had 'made it' in the colonies.

The Imperial also found favour with the highest in the land. The Prince of Wales, the future King Edward VII, became a frequent visitor. Several times he arrived by sea on board the royal yacht, enjoying the fishing in Torbay. His visits to the hotel became especially frequent during the two years his two sons, Albert Victor and George, were at the Britannia Naval College at Dartmouth. He took them there in October 1877, often visited them and took them out in Torquay for theatre or circus, and inevitably for meals to The Imperial, where the Prince himself nearly always stayed. On one such visit the two young princes and their father had afternoon tea with Dean Stanley who was also staying at the hotel (3 April 1878).

Another time in the same year, 'the Prince of Wales arrived on board his yacht and, accompanied by Lord Churston and Sir Henry Seale, witnessed a wrestling match at Dartmouth. Then he proceeded up the River Dart, visited Totnes, Berry Pomeroy and Lupton and returned to the Imperial Hotel.' A few days later, during the same visit, he was rowed to a nearby beach and greatly enjoyed an *al fresco* tea in the garden of the Cary Arms. Alas, to the chagrin of mine host there was no cream in the house, as it was customary for the usual visitors to bring their own. 'It happened however'—we read in one of

IMPERIAL HOTEL,

TORQUAY.

THIS HOTEL, OPEN FOR FAMILIES AND GENTLEMEN,

AFFORDS

Accommodation unequalled in the West of England.

LADIES' COFFEE ROOM, READING ROOM, BILLIARD ROOM, &c.

SOUTH ASPECT.   SEA VIEW.

Near the Baths, Beacon Hill, and the Club.

OMNIBUSES AND FLYS MEET THE TRAINS.

TABLE D'HÔTE AT SEVEN O'CLOCK.

GEORGE HUSSEY,

MANAGER.

An advertisement published in 1878

the books of contemporary history—'that Mrs. Susan Ball and some
friends were enjoying a picnic and were provided with that and other
requisites, which they at once offered to share with the royal party, of
whose rank and position they were ignorant. The offer was accepted in
the most gracious manner by the Prince himself. After tea the party
returned to the Imperial Hotel by launch. Before leaving the Prince
expressed to the manager his pleasure at the visit and said that he was
charmed with the hotel and its lovely situation.'

During his numerous visits, many times the Prince of Wales was
rowed from the yacht direct to the hotel, where the steps cut into the
cliffside lead to a small landing place. This was specially improved by
the hotel management and named, with permission of His Royal
Highness, 'The Prince of Wales's Steps'. The landing has been known
under that name to this day and is used by dinghies and small
launches.

We have precious little information on record regarding the actual
way of life among the guests—and staff—during those glorious
Victorian decades. Obviously, the clients were the 'best people', who
must have had every available comfort in their own homes and would
have expected facilities at least as good, if not better, in their favourite
hotel. On the other hand, in that era one would not have mentioned
the subject of hygiene, sanitation, plumbing, or what have you.

We have to rely on conjecture and snippets of information gleaned
from the records of other, equivalent establishments of the same period
and draw our own conclusions. For example, we know that the
Langham Hotel, which incorporated all the latest devices of luxury
when it opened in 1865—one year before The Imperial, Torquay—in
London, had room for 500 guests and boasted a hydraulic lift (they
called it 'rising room' at the time), fourteen lavatories and nearly 300
water closets. One can only suppose that the word lavatory had a
different meaning in that context, and we may well ask where the
water closets were situated: attached to the bedrooms or in groups
bunched at the end of corridors. As for baths, I have a strong suspicion
that bathrooms as such were seldom found; a small portable bath was
probably taken to the bedroom and filled with hot water from ewers by
the chambermaids. What were in those days often referred to as 'fixed
baths' seem to have been slow in coming.

On the other hand that guess may be wrong. I have come across an
advertisement announcing the opening of the Hotel Angleterre in
Copenhagen in 1875, which proudly claims '. . . 150 salons and rooms

... all rooms have hot and cold baths and douches ...' Here no mention was made of lavatories or water closets, which leaves us guessing on that aspect. The same advertisement also declares that there is a 'hydraulic lift to all floors'. Three years later, in 1878, there was a tragedy in the Grand Hotel, Paris when 'an early type of passenger lift lost its counterpoise and "bounded up from its well with frightful velocity" from the ground floor to the roof of the building, crushing the lift and killing three of the four people in it.'

Or take another, entirely different aspect of hygiene, that of preserving the freshness and wholesomeness of food, not to mention the cooling of water and other drinks, without any kind of refrigeration being available. It is hard to believe this, but a vast amount of ice was used nevertheless. In an article in the trade magazine *The Caterer* dated 6 April 1878 we read: 'We no longer depend on America for our supply of clear block ice, for Norway has entered the market, and rapidly become our principal source of supply, its remarkable purity, cheapness and abundance forming irresistible recommendations.'

It is hard to imagine today, but blocks of ice weighing from two to three hundredweight were imported by the shipload to Britain's shores; suitably packed, they were distributed to hotels and other users throughout the country, mostly by the railways.

On the other hand, our antecedents, hoteliers and their guests had the advantage of better, more relaxed security and safety conditions. This is borne out by the informal and easygoing way in which the VIPs of the time, including royalty such as the Prince of Wales, lived and travelled all over the place in complete safety. And guests at hotels would not have thought it necessary to lock their rooms. In fact it made quite a stir when a client was robbed while staying at The Imperial and demanded compensation from the management; his claim for £30 was settled in full.

As the closing decades of the great Queen's reign moved on, the Imperial Hotel progressed—not entirely free of trials and tribulations, but on the whole with the dignity of success and prosperity.

In 1875 it was found necessary to make extensive alterations to the drains. The medical officer of health of the local authority expressed his complete satisfaction when the work was finished and the management proudly declared that 'The Imperial holds a unique position in sanitary arrangements; probably the best in the country.' However, the size of the dividend had to be reduced for the year owing to the cost of the work, which amounted to £600.

It will be recalled that the site of the hotel was held by the company on a ninety-nine-year lease granted in 1863 at a ground rent of £60 per annum. After much negotiation the freehold of the hotel was bought from the Haldon estate for £3,500 in 1886, and debentures were issued to meet the cost.

At about the same time the thought of expansion was brought to the minds of the directors, when the idea of keeping up with the times made the installation of a lift desirable. The American Elevator Company's representative from London attended the board of directors and estimated the cost to be about £700. The plan was shelved at first, pending the consideration of more ambitious plans of extending the building by the addition of a new block of bedrooms and a billiard and smoking room. All this was eventually approved and the work was put in hand—including the lift—in the year of the Queen's Golden Jubilee.

The advance of science and technology did not leave The Imperial untouched. In March 1887 it was decided to ask the postmaster to establish a branch telegraph office there. On the other hand, when a letter from the District Manager of the Telephone Company was read to the directors at one of their meetings, asking the company to become subscribers to the local exchange, 'the consideration of the question was deferred'. To strike a lighter note, another letter read to the directors must be mentioned; in this one the Clerk of the Local Board stated 'that a complaint had been made of the emission of black smoke from the kitchen chimney of the hotel . . .' It was resolved that the Company Secretary should reply 'that the Directors would make enquiries to see what could be done to remedy the evil complained of'.

It may have nothing to do with the black smoke, but it is amusing to reflect on the fallibility of the press of the period, a long, long time before the term 'media' was needed. In the 1880s an important West Country newspaper reported that *The Lancet* in a leading article recommended Torquay as a 'seductive resort'. In fact, the much respected, learned journal of the medical profession did nothing of the sort; it called Torquay a 'sedative resort'! However, the black smoke from the kitchen chimney suggests that most, if not all, the cooking was done over coal or coke fires, as in most places at that time, although we learn from the company records that the hotel was a large consumer of gas by the year 1890. Using the amount of gas consumed and large amount paid for it as an argument, the Gas Company was approached with a request for a discount. The directors understood this was granted 'to large consumers of gas in other towns'.

A suggestion to introduce electric lighting in the hotel was first discussed at a meeting of the directors in 1893. An electrical engineer in Westminster was asked to come down to inspect the hotel and prepare plans and estimates for electrification. He charged £20 for his expenses for several days, including his rail fares.

The subject of health was not neglected. A list of six names of doctors practising in Torquay was chosen by the board to be given to the Manager—George Hussey at the time—for recommendation to the guests. One of the six was Dr Cash, a homeopathist while another, a Dr Richardson, was elected a director of the company shortly afterwards. Incidentally, when the death of poor Mr Hussey's wife was reported to the board, he was asked to continue as manager at a salary of £200 and authorised to appoint a housekeeper at £50 per annum. This was a temporary solution only, as the posts of manager and manageress were advertised less than two years later. The directors had the unenviable task of selecting from 185 applications. They chose Mr and Mrs F. Fischer, who had previously managed the Hotel d'Europe, Singapore and the Grand Oriental Hotel, Colombo. Appointed from July 1895, their combined remuneration was to be £150 per annum, plus a commission of $2\frac{1}{2}$ per cent on the profits.

The couple took over at a difficult time. Trade had gone down in the preceding year or two, and the very hard frosts in January and February 1895 had reduced the number of first-class passengers on trains as well as the number of guests at the hotel. At the AGM in 1895 the poor results were partly attributed to the lack of sufficient advertising and partly to the less than satisfactory condition of the hotel. Only preferential shares were voted a dividend, ordinary shareholders getting nothing.

Matters were not helped by what today would be described as a takeover battle which broke out towards the end of the year 1895. The attack was led by a hotelier named Kossuth Hudson, who had been managing hotels previously on the Riviera, and a year later took charge of the Coburg Hotel in London (renamed the Connaught during the first world war). His offer to buy The Imperial Hotel outright had to be put before the shareholders at a specially convened extraordinary general meeting, the details of the offer having been given in a circular. At the meeting, which could be described as stormy, there was a great deal of argument for and against the sale and no decision was reached. At an adjourned and not less turbulent meeting, the motion to sell was defeated on a show of hands and afterwards carried on a poll.

The fat was in the fire. Even the directors were unable to agree among themselves, for it must have been tempting for some of them to turn their investment into hard cash. However not all was lost. With the aid of lawyers, including a well known QC, some serious flaws and objections were found and the bid finally repelled.

The stormy meetings over the matter of selling the hotel produced a side issue of battles between the hoteliers of the town—fortunately only in the correspondence columns of the local paper. The Chairman, the Hon E. A. Palk, referring to the improved drainage, let slip the careless remark: 'We have obtained a sanitary certificate—the only one held by a Torquay Hotel.' This was later withdrawn as being incorrect, but the quarrel by correspondence on the subject of 'a new and most perfect system of drainage' continued in the newspaper's columns for several weeks, between the Secretary of the Victoria and Albert Hotel and F. Fischer, Manager of the Imperial Hotel.

When the dust settled the hotel stepped up its advertising effort; this was seen in the best position on the front page of *The Torquay Directory*:

TORQUAY   THE IMPERIAL HOTEL

Under entirely new management. Patronised by English and Continental Royal Families.

THE IMPERIAL is the largest and best situated hotel in Torquay, and the best Winter Residence on the South Coast. It has full south aspect, is completely sheltered from the north and east winds, has a magnificent and uninterrupted view of the whole of Torbay (the English Bay of Naples) and stands in its own private grounds of several acres. The Terrace Walk is over a quarter of a mile in length, close to the sea, with sunny aspect and sheltered from cold winds. New sanitary arrangements throughout on the newest and most approved principles just completed at a cost of approaching £2,000. Plans and certificates can be seen in the fine Entrance Hall.

Special terms made with visitors staying for long periods.

F. Fischer   Manager (late of Singapore and Colombo).

Who would associate the idea of a fashion show with the Victorian era? They are very much part of life in the late twentieth century at The Imperial and elsewhere. There is evidence in the following advertisement that such shows took place from time to time at our favourite hotel as early as 1895–6:

REDFERN

Artists in ladies dress, Cowes
at The Imperial Hotel Torquay today,
Wednesday February 19th

Fresh Spring Models in Gowns, Jackets, Suits and Millinery. Mr. Redfern brings with him an experienced Fitter so that ladies giving orders may be fitted in the Hotel and have their garments finished at any date they may wish.

Redfern, Cowes

Other establishments: London, Paris, New York, Edinburgh and Manchester.

The Fischers were a pronounced success. During the time the new drainage was being installed, guests were disturbed and inconvenienced, mainly by noise from the work, and receipts fell considerably; but after it was all finished, under the new management, the former prosperity returned. The negotiations for the sale of the hotel having failed, repairs, renewals and fresh decorations were carried out and—significantly—a resident plumber was engaged.

News of the zeal and efficiency of the new couple spread like wildfire among the guests and friends of the hotel, and was put on the record by

Outside the main entrance at about the turn of the century

The Torquay Directory, 19 August 1896: 'Old sayings that "new brooms sweep clean" ... the way The Imperial has undergone new management well illustrates this. From top to bottom and bottom to top Mr and Mrs Fischer—the new managers—have had every nook and cranny painted and papered ... Richness and warmth everywhere. The Imperial had for some years been under a cloud as it had not been maintained as it should have been with the result that the shareholders and Torquay were the poorer ... Bright new future dawning ...'

Other promotional ideas cropped up from time to time. At one point it was decided to reduce the charges for carriages, and the rate was fixed to be 2s (10p) to the railway station. Another suggestion was to approach the Great Western Railway asking them to offer tickets (presumably from London) including a week's stay at the Hotel at 6 guineas (£6.30) first class and 5 guineas (£5.25) second during the off-season (May to October). Alas, the Railway Company declined the suggestion.

At a meeting of the board in March 1898 it was decided that 'the electric light be not introduced into the upper floors of the Jubilee Wing, nor into the Table d'Hote Room, but the hall and corridor and the smoking and billiard room be lighted by electricity'. Another great positive step towards a bright future for the hotel was the purchase of the property adjoining it on the west side, for the sum of £10,000 This was the Villa Marina, which was to become some time in the future the West Wing of The Imperial. For the time being the newly acquired property was let at a profitable rent. Before the year was out an offer was received for the sale of the whole property, the hotel and the Marina, for £109,000. In the end the sale did not materialise but the Villa Marina was sold later at a small profit. The century went out on a muted note: the Boer War was not good for business.

4

Into the Twentieth Century

4

The turn of the century could be regarded as a milestone in the progress of the world—for better or worse—and The Imperial in it. The pace of technical advance in all its aspects, especially communications, was to accelerate with tremendous effect on the lives of ordinary and not so ordinary people, and there were shattering upheavals to come.

At the hotel the Boer War made itself felt, however remotely, bringing a small decline in the number of visitors. At the beginning of 1900 the company made a donation of £25 towards the opening of Villa Syracusa as a convalescent home in Torquay for the reception of wounded soldiers, sailors and marines invalided home from South Africa. Opened in February 1900 and closed in December 1901, it looked after 255 invalided servicemen.

At the usual annual meeting of the shareholders in June 1902—at which the Chairman, the Hon Edward Palk, was unable to be present as he was still in South Africa 'serving his King and Country' (peace had been declared a week or two earlier)—a decline in business and profit was reported. This was largely the result of the war, during which staff had to be maintained. With the coming of peace there was hope of better things to come, as the hotel was in excellent condition, and the directors expressed their indebtedness for this to Mr Fischer. At the next meeting, a year later, an increase in trading receipts was declared.

The subject of lighting certain parts of the hotel by electricity cropped up again at a board meeting in July 1903. The specifications prepared by a firm of engineers and their tender for lighting the ground floor and the first and second bedroom floors were accepted, subject to the work being carried out under the supervision of the Torquay Borough Electrician. When, a month later, the directors heard that the Borough Electrician declined the honour, and remembering that the work in all probability would 'interfere with the busier time of business in the hotel', it was decided to defer the matter once again.

A sad note was struck in the report of the directors' meeting in March 1904 when it was 'resolved that consequent on Mr Frederick Fischer's ill-health his services as Manager of the hotel be determined by three months notice, and that he be informed of the directors' great regret that protracted illness should now close an excellent service of nearly ten years duration; a service very highly appreciated by the directors.' Subsequently a Mr Worster was appointed Manager.

The supply of electric light appears to have occupied a great deal of time in the directors' deliberations. The selection of electroliers (electric light fittings resembling a chandelier) was entrusted to Mr Cecil S. Wollen, one of the directors—formerly the company's solicitor and its future chairman. After rejecting one tender and accepting that of another firm, the momentous decision was made to extend the electric light to all parts of the building, including the top floor. The current was to be provided by the hotel's own generating plant, which cost £1,148, including a spare armature for the dynamo, and the supplying contractor had to provide 'an absolute silencer to the engine'.

Plans were approved by the board for a new lounge to be built, extending from the 'garden entrance' at the eastern end of the building. Work was put in hand without delay in 1907 and the addition proved a welcome and highly appreciated rendezvous for the guests. It was all the more of a shock for shareholders to learn at their forty-sixth AGM in June 1909 that although the number of guests had increased, profits were down. Questions raised from the floor suggested that perhaps the guests were becoming more abstemious? Perhaps there was something lacking on the part of the management? It is odd to find that the advertisement published every week during the summer of 1909 was for the best part a verbatim repetition of another which had been used by the previous Manager more than a dozen years before in 1895. When Mr Worster wrote to the chairman tendering his resignation as manager, it was accepted—only too readily, one may think—by the board.

A successor was found in the person of Charles W. Hore, who had a distinguished previous career in charge of other hotels in various seaside resorts. He remained at the helm of The Imperial for very nearly thirty years, right up to the beginning of the second world war. In the same year (1910) another important personal change took place. Cecil S. Wollen (mentioned earlier) was elected Chairman of the board of directors, and the Hon Edward A. Palk Deputy Chairman.

The 'New Lounge' built at the garden entrance at the eastern end of the building in
1907–8

A small incident throws a light on the catering side of those days. At
the March 1911 board meeting the Deputy Chairman produced the
previous evening's menu, handed it round his colleagues and
commented that 'the food was good but scanty, especially now when
there are 70 dining'. He also mentioned a complaint he had received
from a guest of overcharging: three people having been charged £2 17s
for their dinner (£2.85). The manager, who was asked to attend,
explained that the dinner was especially ordered for four people, none
of whom was resident. Col Palk drew attention to the small quantity of
whisky sold for 6d (2½p). A whisky decanter was produced and the
proper quantity poured out—a 'noggin'—to the satisfaction of the
directors who declared it to be ample. At the shareholders' meeting the
same year, in answer to a question regarding the profits on wines and
spirits, the Chairman explained that they were very small, and too
many people were drinking 'water, or ginger beer, or ginger ale'. A
local wine-merchant, who was also a shareholder, rose to the occasion:

'Is that not your fault for charging too much?' 'Why?' queried the Chairman. 'Because you charge such extraordinary prices, too much is taken into the hotel by guests!' was the wine-merchant's retort.

To maintain and indeed improve the standards of the hotel was much in the minds of the new manager and the board of directors. In June 1911 several alterations and additions were decided on. Drastic changes to be made in the Jubilee wing, included demolishing it down to the first floor which had to have a new roof; the lavatory accommodation was to be 'largely re-modelled' and further new lavatories provided and private bathrooms were added to all the suites in the hotel.

The use of the motor car had made a significant beginning. The first RAC *Handbook* was published in 1909 and hotels were then 'appointed' by a committee. The AA started appointments a little earlier, and introduced its star system in 1912—The Imperial was rated four star in those early years. The growth of motoring benefited hotel development; the advent of the AA and RAC *Handbooks* was an incentive for hotels to maintain and sustain their standards of amenities and services. Another effect, in the case of The Imperial, was the building of a new 'motor garage' in 1912.

Other improvements were made 'behind the scenes' of the hotel. A new stillroom was constructed and the kitchen was moved from the basement to the ground floor to be next to it, a new electric lift for luggage was installed and more new bathrooms. It was just as well this was done then, because the outbreak of war in 1914 halted, at least temporarily, all further modernisation plans.

In the list of hotels published by *The Torquay Times*—headed by The Imperial—this description was given in the pre-war years:

> THE IMPERIAL HOTEL.—Premier of Torquay. Position un-equalled on the South Coast. Patronised by English and Continental Royal Families. Re-decorated and Re-Furnished. Self-contained Bathroom Suites. Headquarters Royal Automobile Club.—The Imperial is the largest and best situated Hotel in Torquay, and the best Winter Residence on the South Coast. It has full south aspect.—
> C. W. Hore, Manager.

(It should be noted that the term 'Headquarters of the RAC' simply meant that the hotel had been 'appointed' by the club; there was one other in Torquay so honoured, the Grand.)

It was said that the 1914 war ruined the holiday business in seaside resorts. Many German or Austrian staff members in hotels and restaurants, managers and waiters equally, were dismissed or interned; a number of them emigrated to America. Licensing restrictions were imposed, reducing the hours from continuous permitted drinking all day, which had been the previous rule. By 1915 the disastrous war news overshadowed everything; food prices and maintenance costs had risen steeply, there was hardly any banqueting business, and of course no foreign visitors. The scanty records from this period show that the manager was granted two increases of salary during the war, and that in June 1915 the directors resolved 'that having regard to the present state of the war no exceptional repairs or alterations should at present be undertaken.' In 1917 more restrictions were introduced by the authorities. The supply of meat, bread, flour and other foods as well as tea and coffee had to be controlled and there was a 'no treating' order made, forbidding anyone to buy a drink for a friend in any bar. In the last year of the war most food was rationed by the Public Meals Order and meatless days were enforced.

In August 1918 The Imperial narrowly missed being taken over by the military authorities for convalescent officers back from the front;

The corridor lounge, still showing its full, original splendour, photographed during the early part of this century

several other hotels had been requisitioned. The hotel had been inspected with this in view, but no decision was taken before the war ended.

There was much to be done after the Armistice and the next few years saw progress in many aspects of the hotel's amenities. Several public rooms, the dining-room, entrance hall and 'corridor lounge', were badly in need of redecorating and refurnishing. The dining-room was found to need enlarging, to be achieved partly by removing four solid, space-consuming pillars. For good measure, the room was also given a kind of minstrels' gallery, used for many years to come by a trio or quartet playing soft music for the diners. The smoking-room was enlarged by taking in the space occupied by the ladies' lavatory next door, and a new ladies' lavatory was constructed elsewhere.

A new electric lift to all floors was installed by Waygood Otis and the very progress-conscious manager, Mr Hore, urged the directors that it was time the hotel had a motor bus. In those early post-war years most visitors arrived by train and were met at the station by the hotel's horse-drawn omnibus and coachman. A 30–35 horsepower Vauxhall chassis was bought and fitted with a 'first class and suitable body', at a total cost of £800; this could not have been a complete success, for only a year later (1920) the Chairman was authorised to visit the Motor Show and buy a new bus at about £1,275.

The neighbouring villa, the Marina, was repurchased by the company in 1921, a covered corridor built to connect it with the main building and finally converted into further accommodation of suites and rooms, it became the 'west wing'. In the former Marina's grounds a hard and a grass tennis court were made.

The west wing had hot and cold water provided in every room with a 'screen to each basin enabling any room to be used as a sitting-room'. Each room was heated by an 'eight-section radiator' and a special boiler was installed to supply the additional heating. On the north (landward) side of the corridor further rooms were built for the use of visitors' maids.

Owing to illness, Col Palk had to resign his position as a director and Deputy Chairman in 1925; the board accepted this with great regret, but resolved that the vacancy should not be filled. A year later, Thomas Henry Green, Company Secretary for the previous twenty-six

(*previous page*) The Imperial with its clifftop gardens, about 1925

View from the Beacon, about 1925

years, died and the board appointed as Secretary C. J. H. (John) Wollen, the Chairman's son. He continued later as a director, and finally (from 1947) became the last Chairman before the company became part of Trust Houses in 1969.

Progress continued throughout the twenties under the capable management of Charles Hore, who was highly regarded by all concerned. He also excelled in public life, became a town councillor and Mayor of Torquay in 1927–28. He was greatly assisted in the management of The Imperial by his wife; in fact many people thought that it was her ability and vision that was of particular benefit to the hotel. Her husband himself must have regarded her as the 'power behind the throne', for when she died, sometime in the mid-twenties, he had an imposing monument erected on her grave and described her as 'The Imperial Queen' in her epitaph.

Times were changing with more and more momentum. A charming lady, now in her eighties, who worked in the hotel offices from 1918–25 recollects some details of the life-style: 'Cars were beginning to come on the scene and visitors brought their cars and chauffeurs . . . the hotel was busiest from November to April, when there were never any vacancies . . . Whole families used to come from Scotland and the North of England, who would stay sometimes the whole season, or a good part of it, and return each year.' 'Three resident musicians, who played for tea daily and also after dinner in the evenings and for concerts and dances . . . during Christmas and New Year entertainers came from London . . .'

55

The age of the motor car was indeed upon us by the end of the twenties. As mentioned earlier, hotels had been 'appointed' by the two motoring organisations for a number of years. The Automobile Association started its award of stars in 1912, and The Imperial was first among the four-star hotels until 1921, when for some reason it lost one for a couple of years. From 1922–25 it was classified as four star again, until it received the fifth star which it has retained ever since. The RAC did not introduce the star system until 1951, when The Imperial was rated as four star ('first class hotels . . . comfort above the ordinary'); the five-star category was introduced in 1955 and The Imperial was among the first eight hotels in the UK to join it.

Life was still elegant and formal; people still expected to change for the evening, and this was *de rigueur* at The Imperial as much as in the West End of London. When an Australian tourist complained that he could not dine out in the better hotels or restaurants of London without wearing evening dress, the magazine *The Caterer* made this comment: 'We cannot understand any man wanting to participate in a function where men and women are in evening dress, clad in plus fours, Oxford bags or a rainbow-coloured suit. It is not done in England . . .'

In other respects the *mores* were changing towards the end of the twenties. Whereas so far we have not found any mention of locks and bolts on hotel room doors—evidently because nobody saw any need for them—in 1929 The Imperial's management had to invest a considerable sum on a supply of locks, keys and bolts for the doors of all the rooms. One cannot help wondering why this had become not only desirable, but probably necessary.

On a more progressive note, before the end of 1929 the electrician's room at The Imperial was converted into an electricity sub-station and the change over to the Corporation electricity supply was completed.

5

Life in the Thirties

5

Members of royal families continued to use The Imperial in the 1930s. Early in April 1931 Princess Beatrice, the King's aunt, went there to complete her convalescence from an acute attack of bronchitis, which had developed after she had broken her left arm through slipping in one of her rooms at Kensington Palace.

The following month she was visited at the hotel by ex-King Alfonso (of Spain), accompanied by his third son, Prince Juan, on his way to join the RN College at Dartmouth as a naval cadet. The ex-monarch's visit was to be a private one, but news of it had leaked out and crowds gathered at the railway station and outside The Imperial—in spite of the fact that inquirers at the hotel were not encouraged but simply told: 'We know nothing.'

The visitor was very popular in Britain and was given a tremendous ovation when met at the station by Princess Beatrice who came in her own royal Daimler from the hotel. They did not drive straight to the hotel but took a long detour through Newton Abbot and Dartmoor, returning about two hours later. As no one knew the exact time of arrival, the crowd at The Imperial had waited and showed no loss of enthusiasm, when the moment came. Inside the vestibule Charles Hore was also kept waiting before he was able to greet the royal guests and escort them to the lift. They went straight to the suite occupied by the Princess, which was facing south/south-west and when the King looked out over the bay he was said to have exclaimed: 'What a glorious view!' The royal party had tea there before the King went to his own suite, then named after Napoleon III, who had occupied it for five weeks sixty years before.

Time marched on and in step with it the growing needs and demands of hotel guests. In December 1933 the manager submitted to the board of directors several letters from intending guests—some of many years standing—declaring that they would not book accommodation because there was no central heating throughout the hotel. It was agreed that central heating had become essential. Mr Wollen took the opportunity to propose another far-seeing project.

'J' Class yachts racing in Torbay during the 'Fortnight' in 1935, with The Imperial in the background

At that time the best, sea-facing part of the ground floor, the area between the famous red plush 'corridor lounge' and the south facade of the building, was occupied by some of the best suites of the hotel. Now the chairman revealed his plan to demolish these suites to form one large lounge-ballroom, which would make the most of the superb view over a magnificent terrace. He also suggested creating more single bedrooms with private baths and that all these works, including total central heating, should be carried out at the same time. He won the day.

The new 'Sun Lounge & Ballroom' was formally opened on 22 March 1935. The souvenir programme and menu provides a detailed account of this feast and a fairly complete impression of the lifestyle of the upper and upper middle classes in the thirties, including their habits as regards food, wine and entertainment. The Chairman and directors received the guests from 6.30 to 7 pm, during this time soft music being provided by Emilio Colombo and his orchestra—they were brought down from London for the occasion, and the programme consisted of excerpts from musical comedies and operas, from Lehar to Puccini, haunting Viennese Valses, souvenirs of Naples and gipsy Russian airs. Similar music was played by the resident Imperial Hotel Orchestra during the banquet, which was timed to begin at 7 o'clock.

The menu was lavish and must have been most carefully put together, while the wines offered would raise a certain amount of envy today.

DINER

Perles de Whitstable

Hors d'Oeuvres Choisis   Barquettes de Caviar

* * *

Tortue des Indes au Xeres

Velouté de Volaille Juanita

* * *

Darne de Saumon d'Ecosse Pochée

Sauce Marguery

* * *

Mignonettes d'Agneau à la Cussy

Pommes Nouvelles   Haricots au Beurre

* * *

Poussins de Printemps Rôti au Lard

Salade Niçoise

* * *

Asperges Vertes de Lauri   Sauce Mousseline

* * *

Charlotte à la Russe   Bombe Georgette

Friandises

* * *

Paillettes au Parmesan

* * *

Dessert

* * *

Café

The imposing array of wines started with sherry, Amontillado 'Alvado' (one could assume that this was served during the reception). With the first few courses came a white wine, Château La Flora Blanche (it is hard to tell what this would have been like) and the red wine with the main courses was a mature, solid Beaune 1921. Following the French custom which must have been ruling in Britain at the time, dinner ended with a vintage champagne: Irroy, Carte d'Or, Extra Quality 1923. Here too, it was customary to drink champagne with much more bottle age than we prefer today.

An artist's impression of the newly opened ballroom and sun lounge, 1935

The port was Dow's 1920, which must have reached a perfect condition; it was described by the late H. Warner Allen as an 'elegant, very attractive wine'. The list of liqueurs was headed by Courvoisier's VVO (forty years old—where would one find anything like it today?) and offered a choice of nine distinguished names. Cigars and cigarettes were also on offer.

'The King' was followed by a toast to 'The Imperial Hotel' proposed by Sir John Foster Fraser, the guest of honour and seconded by the Mayor of Torquay. Response was by C. S. Wollen, Chairman of the directors.

'A Dance & Cabaret', 9 pm to 2 am, followed the banquet with the 'personal appearance of Emilio Colombo and his Band'. The following appeared in cabaret at midnight: Valerie Lavall and Michael Woolley (of Grosvenor House, Park Lane), who gave an exhibition of ballroom dances (Old Fashioned Waltz, Quick Step, Slow Fox Trot and Rumba); James Stewart, 'The Tramp Pianist', entertained and Herbert Milton presented his 'Magic Extraordinary'. No doubt a good time was had by all. The excellent sketch showing the dancing in progress in the new ballroom reveals that all the gentlemen, without exception, wore white tie and tails.

Shortly after this heartening event, Charles Hore, Manager of the hotel since 1910, was appointed Managing Director. The work of adding more private bathrooms and improving the cloakrooms and lavatories continued; at a meeting on 11 October 1935 'the construction of two squash courts outside the dining room was considered and it was resolved that scaffolding to be erected to show whether the elevation would in any way interfere with the view from the dining room windows.' It didn't and they went ahead with the plan. The courts were in use by the following year.

Christmas has always been a specially busy time at The Imperial and it was so in 1935, judging by the report in *The Torquay Times*:

A Bumper Christmas in the old fashioned way . . .

'Never has The Imperial been as full as it is this year. I am told that the guests are staying longer than usual this year.

'There have been tennis, table tennis and billiards tournaments, bridge drives, entertainments by Mr Will Kings, the well known London society entertainer and gala dances. A real old fashioned Christmas party spirit of Yuletide was recaptured. On Boxing Night there was a very successful Fancy Dress Ball when some novel and interesting costumes were seen.

'Councillor Charles Hore, the Managing Director told me that they had several distinguished guests including Sir Edward Nicholl and his family, Sir Ernest and Lady Shenthall, Mr Julius Hagen (film director at Elstree) and Mr M. Lyons, K.C., M.P.'

Two or three weeks later the same reporter wrote (22 January 1936):'Mr. Charles Hore the managing director of the Imperial Hotel showed me several letters of appreciation received . . . in one of these a gentleman wrote from the North of England: "There is only one more comfortable place than my own fireside, and that is a room in the West Wing of the Imperial Hotel".'

In June 1936 Lady Astor paid a short visit to receive a tumultuous welcome; among others staying at The Imperial at the same time were the Rt Hon Oliver Stanley and Sir Henry Pelham. A note of optimism was prevalent at the AGM later the same month. The Chairman was able to report 'a happy state of affairs', describing the improvements and additions including the 'run of bedroom-bathroom suites opened for the first time last Easter'. The views expressed by guests on these and the new lounge and balcony adjoining it 'were most gratifying'.

Later that year the hotel company made a donation of £100 towards the cost of the International Coronation Regatta to be held in

Torbay in 1937. Early in 1937 it was decided to engage a professional to coach guests in squash and tennis at a salary of 30s. (£1.50) per week (to live in). To put his salary in perspective, a fulltime painter's wage at the same time was 3 guineas (£3.15), not living in, of course.

In 1937 the International Coronation Regatta attracted a magnificent display of sail and the spacious new terrace adjoining the new ballroom-lounge made a superb vantage point for watching it. Although the legendary 'J' Class had disappeared since the previous season, there were six 12 metres entered, as well as fifteen yachts in the over 75 ton handicap and twenty-five in the 25–75 ton classes. Further there were seven 8 metres and eight 6 metres entered and an eyewitness rightly remarked: 'We shall hardly see the like again.'

Many leading personalities of the yachting world made their headquarters at The Imperial and entertained lavishly. The Managing Director was congratulated by his own directors on the many compliments received from the leading yachtsmen on the excellence of the various lunches and dinners served.

New kitchen equipment, including refrigeration, was installed and telephone extensions in the rooms, requiring a new switchboard for the hotel. In March 1938 a musical broadcast was first arranged from The Imperial, at a fee of £50. A five-piece band had been engaged for the preceding winter led by Cliff Gwilliams (previously at Rhyl) who must have been the broadcasters of 'Palm Court' type of music. The total cost to the hotel of the five players was £29 per week, and when a sixth, an additional first violinist, joined them his pay amounted to 30s (£1.50) per week. In the summer of 1938 new equipment for floodlighting the hotel was introduced . . . no one thought at the time that it would not be functioning very long.

6

The Imperial Goes to War

6

After Munich, as the storm clouds were gathering, foreshadowing the cataclysm of the second world war, a general foreboding and feeling of uneasiness spread among every section of the population in Britain. At the beginning of the year 1939 the Chief Air Raid Warden of the district visited the hotel to discuss the possible precautions to be taken there if war should come. Among other suggestions the use of the squash courts as an air-raid shelter for 200 people was proposed.

Fearing the worst, several large business concerns were endeavouring to make arrangements to evacuate from London and other centres to places of supposed safety, such as Torquay. One of the largest insurance companies opened negotiations with The Imperial for a ten-year option to be able to take over the hotel 'in the event of a war crisis'. The offer was later withdrawn as the insurance company decided that the hotel's overheads were too heavy to contemplate the arrangement.

Come the time of the last pre-war AGM—in June, as usual— the results reported were depressing: 'Almost complete stagnation since last autumn has marked the business and holiday side of our country's life.' Other circumstances had been equally unsatisfactory: 'Bad weather . . . roads impassable to cars . . . kept clients away at Christmas . . .'

By midsummer the local paper was reporting on the precautions taken by the various hotels against war contingencies in Torquay. Citing The Imperial as a fine example of wisdom and foresight, the report concluded: 'One hopes that the rest of Torquay hotels are following this example and "taking all steps necessary and proper" for the purpose of guarding staff and visitors from injury from Air Raids.'

Within a few days of the declaration of war a blow fell which was not totally unexpected by the management and the directors of the hotel. At their meeting on 14 September the Chairman reported that The Imperial Hotel would very probably be requisitioned by the Air Ministry; he had been unable to get anything definite out of the ministry official who had been inspecting the premises with a view to turning them into a training centre for Air Force cadets.

A couple of days later—things were moving fast—a formal requisition was received from the Lands Officer, Air Ministry, signed on behalf of the responsible Minister. This was to be acknowledged by the Chairman, who was to point out the difficulties of the hotel arising from the problem of finding accommodation for the furniture and equipment, which was not expected to be needed by the Ministry. From this request arose the Ministry's suggestion that the top storey of the building could be excluded from the requisition and used for the storage of all the furniture, or at least as much of it as was possible with regard to the safety of the building. The hotel's architect was asked whether the structure was strong enough for all the furniture to be stored in the top storey; he expressed serious doubts.

Nothing could halt the grinding-on of the wartime bureaucracy; relentlessly, a notice was served on the hotel, dated 19 September, with a request in accordance with the Defence Regulations in force to arrange the evacuation of all hotel guests within seven days. The Chairman was obliged to send a letter to each of the guests explaining the position and informing them that to the board's regret the hotel would not be available after 28 September 1939.

Further action by the management had to be swift. The wine merchant who had been a regular supplier for many years, agreed to take back all the 'light wines' and to store the others, not subject to deterioration, for the duration of the war. Notice was given to members of the staff, terminating their employment as from 30 September. Each of them was given any holidays on full pay that were due, plus one month's pay from the date of the notice. No exception was made in the case of the Managing Director, C. W. Hore, who was given notice terminating his contract with the company at the end of six months. 'The Chairman paid a sincere tribute with which each member of the Board in turn associated himself, to the work that Mr Hore had done for the hotel during the many years of his association with it; to have to terminate this association was the most painful of all the duties forced upon the Board by the requisitioning of the hotel by the Government.'

All was not lost however. The directors, and the Chairman in particular, continued their efforts to save the hotel from requisitioning, or at least from as much of the damage as possible. No stone was left unturned. At one stage joint consultations took place with the owner of the Grand Hotel, which found itself in a similar position. Together they took Counsel's opinion as to the legality or otherwise of the requisitioning itself and the way it had been carried out—without avail. Together they also sought the intervention of the local Member of Parliament with the Air Ministry, to seek the withdrawal of the requisition, or at least some assistance in the disposal of the hotel's furniture not required by the Ministry.

In spite of all these efforts, the final demand from the authorities for the handing over on 6 October was issued. It became clear that there would not be any space left in the hotel building for the storage of any furniture, etc and a lease had to be taken on a substantial house in the town for storing goods for the duration. A caretaker was employed there to look after the company's property. Then—almost a miracle— the unexpected happened and the requisition was withdrawn.

This volte-face was never fully explained. It was thought at the time that perhaps a change of policy took place in the Air Ministry and it was decided that young cadets could be better managed, organised and looked after in smaller units, such as boarding houses and small hotels. The outcome was that by mid-October the hotel had been handed back to the owners, albeit as an empty shell, and the directors also had the problem of having no staff and no Manager. The chairman asked a member of the D'Oyly Carte family who had an estate in the vicinity if through the connection with the Savoy Hotel, he could help him to find someone suitable. The Savoy management indeed was able to recommend a talented young hotelier who was well known to them, as the son of their former Manager, right from the beginning of his career in the business.

H. M. Chapman—better known everywhere as Michael Chapman—went straight into the hotel industry after leaving his public school. His training was comprehensive; he worked in all departments of hotels in Austria, France, Germany and Switzerland, and having returned to England in various capacities at the Savoy, the Berkeley and Claridges. He got his first chance in management in Edinburgh, followed by another in Inverness. Back in Edinburgh, he had opened a new hotel only a short time before the outbreak of war, and as luck would have it this was requisitioned, so he happened to be free when the call from Torquay came.

He went to Torquay for an interview with the Chairman and directors, was thoroughly inspected and in turn had a chance to tour the great hotel, sadly empty, deprived of contents and guests. They must have clicked: members of the board must have sensed the promise of enterprise combined with the right kind of worldly experience, and the young applicant must have felt the challenge presented to him by the potentially great hotel.

By 29 October all was ready and The Imperial Hotel was opened under its new Manager, and with all the staff that could be reassembled. When Michael Chapman saw the furnishings as they were brought back from storage, he felt strongly that some were much too old-fashioned and should be replaced as soon as possible. He still remembers with a shudder the prevalence of brass bedsteads and other monstrosities. At that time, not only was money a little tight, but it was getting difficult to find what was wanted. Supplies became more and more restricted as the war progressed. But life and business at the hotel picked up after the reopening, and it was almost 'business as usual', at least while the 'phoney war' lasted.

At the beginning of December a fashion show at The Imperial was followed by a bridge drive, which raised over £100 for a good cause, comforts for merchant seamen. For the opening of the Christmas festivities, on the 23rd a dinner and dance was advertised at 12s 6d (62½p), or dance only at 5s (25p). On Christmas Night there was a Grand Gala Fancy Dress Ball, with crackers and balloons, at 21s (£1.05), another party on Boxing Night, a Children's Christmas Party during the week, on the 30th an Economy Dance—complete costume not to exceed 2s 6d (12½p), and on New Year's Eve there was an Orchestral Concert, followed by a 'Brilliant Spectacular Heralding the New Year . . .'

Conditions were not getting any easier now, and hardships began to bite. Rationing started in January 1940 with butter, sugar and bacon, extending to meat in March and tea, margarine and other cooking fats in July. Enforcing the blackout posed another problem. When the Manager reported this to the board, they authorised him to arrange for patrolling the grounds during the night, so as to ensure compliance. In June 1940 an offer by the ARP authorities to establish two posts at the hotel, to be manned by volunteers from the staff, was agreed.

After Dunkirk, when the RAF Initial Training Wing was moved from Hastings to Torquay, Michael Chapman agreed to take thirty officers at half a guinea (52½p) a day. This helped to maintain occupancy at the hotel and a further, powerful stimulus was given to business with the beginning of the serious bombing raids on London. People started flocking to The Imperial seeking respite and a safe refuge from the blitz. During the autumn of 1940, Michael Chapman reported to the board that 'owing to the continued increase in business, it would be a great help in the running of the hotel if he could have an assistant manager' and he was duly empowered to engage one.

Business was flourishing during this period, in spite of the inevitable hardships imposed by war conditions. Early in 1941 a large part of the lawn in front of the West Wing was dug up and turned into a vegetable garden. It was about the same time that a hairdressing and beauty salon as well as a barber shop was installed. The hotel had contracts with some farmers in the surrounding countryside who supplied chickens in return for leftovers to be used as chicken-feed; nothing was to be wasted.

In a public-spirited way the management discouraged long-stay guests during the war, on the principal that the greatest number of people should enjoy a holiday as a relief from the stresses and strains which affected everyone, in one way or another, during wartime. One of the very few exceptions was the legendary Eugene Higgins, the American multi-millionaire. He had been living in France, having owned substantial homes in Paris and the Riviera, but was caught by the outbreak of war while cruising in the English Channel on board his large, luxury yacht, and put into the nearest safe haven, which happened to be Torquay. The vessel was requisitioned by the Admiralty early in 1940, and the obvious solution was to move into The Imperial, where he stayed for several years, even after the war, in fact until he died.

A true eccentric, Mr Higgins became a well-known figure among hotel guests who derived much amusement from his often odd behaviour. His entourage consisted of his equally eccentric French lady friend—thought to have been nearer seventy than sixty—and his secretary, M Cousteau, who had left his wife and young son in France; the latter was to grow up to become the famous under-water explorer.

Michael Chapman remembers some of Higgins's eccentricities with amusement to this day: his obsession with his health, resulting in vast numbers of pills surrounding him at table, his attention to detail—M Cousteau had to keep a written record of every air-raid warning for him, and telephone the BBC if Big Ben on the radio was sounded 2–3 seconds late. Mme Chapelle, the lady friend, had her own eccentricities, one of them that she tried to hide the fact that her feet were not the same size and she had to buy two different pairs of shoes. Guests were enthralled to watch the nightly spectacle of the Higgins party's arrival in the dining-room.

First at the table was Higgins himself in an old-fashioned frock-coat with a fresh buttonhole. On arrival he immediately helped himself to two pats of butter out of three provided (one each was the ration). Next came Mme Chapelle, greatly over-dressed in heavy make-up, and took her place at the table, helping herself to the remaining butterpat.

When finally poor Cousteau joined the table, he found he had to do without butter. When old Higgins died, he had willed his whole fortune—said to be close on £200 million—to be divided between the three leading universities in the US. His nieces and nephews had to be content with small legacies of $1,000 each. Some of the disappointed relatives attempted to upset the will on grounds of his insanity, but failed: it was established in law that Mr Higgins might have been very, very eccentric, as confirmed by many witnesses, but was basically of sound mind.

Even The Imperial could not escape the direct effect of the war for ever. Damage was inflicted on it in a bombing raid during the summer of 1941. All the carefully prepared precautions worked as planned, no one was injured and the damage to buildings was luckily only superficial. Special tribute was paid to Mr Chapman and his staff for the way 'they have risen to the occasion and worked really splendidly'. The guests who had been coming to the hotel in order to escape from London and elsewhere ever since the 'blitz' started were on the move again after the bombing incident. However, business remained brisk, for there were not many places left in the South of England where such enjoyable holidays could be had.

Broadcasts of music and cabaret had been made at intervals from the hotel, which was much appreciated by radio listeners and also by the guests. At the insistence of the directors no mention was made of the name of the hotel; they felt that 'this form of advertisement was not at present desirable'.

Rationing became more severe in the course of 1942. By June, hotels and restaurants became subject to the drastic 'Meals in Establishments Order', which limited a meal to three courses and its price to 5s (25p). Service charges and the prices of drinks served with meals were controlled. The only exceptions were a small extra charge allowed for dancing to live music and/or cabaret. Some luxury establishments were permitted to add a house charge to the bills for meals, up to an additional 6s (30p). Another order issued in September the same year completely prohibited the making of ice cream.

At about the same time all the railings around the hotel and the putting course, also all the ornamental gates, had been removed by the Ministry of Works. The Chairman and the Manager between them managed to persuade the powers that were to leave the main entrance gates to the drive for the time being.

In spite of all the war-related vicissitudes The Imperial continued to excel as an oasis of wellbeing and as much enjoyment as was possible within the limitations of the restrictions. This is the firm impression one gets from the contemporary reports in the press, such as the one in *The Torquay Times* of 6 January 1943:

> Torquay hotels generally seem to have been gayer for the New Year's Eve than they were at Christmas. Possibly the increasingly good news from Russia resulted in people thinking that they were entitled to 'celebrate'.
>
> The Imperial Hotel had over 300 guests for dinner and more joined them for the cabaret and dance. Indeed, but for the preponderance of uniforms, the atmosphere was almost one of peacetime.
>
> In the cabaret the BBC artists Forsythe, Seaman and Farrell appeared in 'A ton of fun' which was to the obvious liking of the guests. Jack Padbury's orchestra, as usual, seemed to play all the right tunes at the right time and everyone was aroused to the proper pitch of expectation when the chimes of midnight began to toll.
>
> Then, 'Old Man 1942' walked with tired steps across the ballroom. As he disappeared into the limbo of the past there came the patter of hoofs from the opposite direction and little 'Miss 1943' rode into the room on a black pony.

'A good show, Mr Chapman!' concluded the writer. On a more intimate and personal level, here is an extract from a letter of a friend, describing some of his wartime experiences while he was stationed near Torquay and frequently sought relaxation at The Imperial: 'It was one of the few if not the only hotel in England where dinner jackets or dress uniform were compulsory. Dancing went on until well after midnight and the war outside seemed far away . . .'

While frequently taking his turn at fire-watching on the roof during air-raids and helping to deal with the odd fire-bomb that fell, the management of the hotel was Mr Chapman's primary concern, and in this he excelled. In fact, his zeal and imagination marked the beginning—even during those difficult war years—of a new era of revival and progress. His achievement as well as his promise was recognised by the Chairman and the board, when at the end of 1943 they appointed him Managing Director of the company. When the war came to an end, under his strong management the hotel was ready and poised for a significant further leap ahead.

7

Expansion and Modernisation

7

The many changes that came, inevitably, to the style of development of The Imperial were the effect of several causes. Without trying to analyse these too deeply at this stage, it becomes obvious that a fundamental change had taken place in the management—one might almost say command—structure, due almost entirely to the character and personality of those involved.

Having studied the records available, right from the beginnings, the impression is gained that it was the directors who were actively in charge, the manager merely carrying out their instructions as a kind of front man. Even the early chairmen of the board did not take an active part; they were mere figureheads.

In one respect, the change took place before the war; we have seen the active involvement of the Chairman, Cecil S. Wollen, during the critical struggle over the requisitioning of the hotel, and this had firmly established his leadership. He proved himself a far-sighted man, looking to the future when he was largely responsible for the appointment of Michael Chapman as Manager, and later as Managing Director. He must have felt that The Imperial had fallen behind and needed revitalising. The new Manager was a very different type of man; compared to his old-fashioned predecessors, he was raring to go—mostly in the right direction—and he was given his head by his provident Chairman.

It is not altogether surprising that a similar attitude was taken by the successor to the chair, for John Wollen had many years as Secretary and later as director, and had worked closely with his father on furthering the interests of the hotel. Both father and son were, in succession, the senior members of a prominent firm of solicitors in Torquay, and their involvement in the hotel business must have given them a great deal of pleasure in return for their dedication.

The change of Chairmen took place at a board meeting on 15 August 1946, when 'the Chairman, Mr. C. S. Wollen, said that he had given much thought to the kind appeal made to him by the Board and by the shareholders to reconsider his decision not to offer himself for reelection as Chairman. He had however with much reluctance decided that after thirty-six years as chairman it was time he handed over the heavy responsibilities of the appointment to a younger man, and he suggested that the Board might consider appointing as his successor Mr. John Wollen, who had been so intimately associated with the administration of the company's business during the past twenty years, first as secretary and later as member of the Board. Each member of the Board in turn expressed his deep regret at hearing Mr. Wollen's decision, and it was resolved that Mr John Wollen be and he was thereby elected Chairman of Directors for the ensuing year.' Cecil Wollen died two years later and his son John continued as Chairman uninterrupted until the hotel was taken over by Trust Houses in the year 1969 ... but that is another story, to be dealt with later.

From the start John Wollen gave his full backing to Michael Chapman, and the two had a lasting relationship of friendship, trust and mutual respect. John Wollen well remembers how, at their first business meeting after he became chairman, Michael Chapman confided that John's father had been a father-figure to him, to whom he had been looking for encouragement and support. He had to readjust to working with a man of his own generation. For close on a quarter of a century, they had regular weekly meetings: every Monday John Wollen arrived for lunch during which, and for two or three hours afterwards, they discussed business thoroughly. This collaboration proved most beneficial and helped the smooth and effective running of board meetings.

Michael Chapman's arrival on the scene did more than stirring all into action; it was a veritable 'wind of change'. Coming freshly from the outside world—from the international hotel scene, in fact—he was able to see with a fresh eye what was wrong and what needed doing. He felt simply that The Imperial had fallen behind. It was still the leading hotel, but mainly for the old-time clientele which had used it in the past, in the days when wealthy people came for winter holidays. He felt that such people would continue to diminish in numbers, and immediately, even during the war, he made every effort to attract younger, more contemporary guests. This, at the beginning, meant extending every possible welcome to members of the forces, by price concessions and suitable entertainment. He rightly considered that such guests would constitute the nucleus of a prosperous post-war business.

At first he found the directors a little old-fashioned, perhaps even parochial, in their outlook, but it did not take him too long to win them over. As an example, they agreed that The Imperial should have a bar open to the public, with direct access from outside. He thought that the state of the bedrooms was 'worn' and was able to get the board's co-operation; led by the Chairman, they became anxious to help with making improvements. Much redecorating was needed as well as refurnishing. Chapman remembers the old brass bedsteads he found, which 'rattled'; they were replaced by wooden ones, and new wardrobes were bought as soon as possible, although the idea of built-in furniture had not arrived. Gradually more and more private bathrooms were created, very often by taking space from the vast old-fashioned bedrooms.

By the end of the war the reputation of the hotel for offering the best of everything—including as good a standard of food as possible—was firmly established. Once more the very top people patronised The Imperial. The late Princess Royal and the Earl of Harewood spent seven weeks and celebrated their Silver Wedding there in 1947 and came to stay again in 1952.

In 1948 the yachting events of the Olympic Games were raced in Torbay, and The Imperial made a superb base for the top helmsmen as well as offering the finest grandstand view to the onlookers; the magnificent terraces, especially the one adjoining the ballroom, came into their own. As one would expect, some of the most important social events connected with the Olympic Regatta were also held at the hotel, such as the 'XIV Olympiad Gala Supper and Ball—to mark the conclusion of the Olympic Yachting'. It must have been a glittering occasion—this was the cold buffet supper:

Le Homard de Torbay Imperial

* * *

Le Chaud-Froid de Volaille à la Gelée de Porto

* * *

La Salade de Laitues et Tomates

* * *

La Mayonnaise de Pommes de Terre

* * *

Le Biscuit Glacé Napolitaine

* * *

La Patisserie Francaise

It must have been about this time that a special description of The Imperial was introduced, to remain a slogan used in publicity and advertising: 'The English Hotel in the Mediterranean Manner'. The English character of the place was further emphasised when Michael Chapman changed the language of all the menus to English. William True, perhaps the most talented of the head chefs ever to work at the hotel, joined in 1951 and he supported this notion whole-heartedly; menus in English have become a unique feature ever since. As to the materials used in the kitchen, conditions were by no means trouble-free; rationing was still in force, to be finally ended in July 1954.

In 1950 Michael Chapman made a tour of the United States, mainly to study the latest developments and ideas in the hotel industry there. One of the many innovations he brought back in his mind resulted in the new Marine restaurant, the opening of which in 1952 represents the first important stage of the complete modernisation, internal and external, of The Imperial.

Here are some of the details, as published in *The Torquay Times* 13 June 1952:

'The new 12ft windows are continuous and lean forward about eighty degrees providing practically an unobstructed view down and across Torbay. A circular hardwood dance floor has been constructed in the centre of the internal section of the dining room, and at each end of this the floor is raised as terraces to provide diners with a view to the sea over the heads of other diners and tables in front . . . A system of ventilation has been installed which delivers filtered fresh air which may be warmed as required . . . by thermostatic control.

'Lighting is provided by a beautiful old English cut glass chandelier . . . by specially designed ceiling fittings and the balance of lighting by table lamps. Plugs have also been installed so that clients can speak on the telephone from their table if required . . .

'In the architects' design simplicity was the keynote . . . decorations have been kept plain, special dressing being left to the furnishings, such as the curtains, carpeting, flower boxes, etc. . . . Ivory venetian sun blinds are provided to the continuous windows . . .

'The very modern design has been made to blend in with the exterior and, at the same time take advantage of the unique setting the hotel enjoys. Patrons may breakfast and lunch whilst enjoying the sights of the yachts and motor craft which ply the harbour and lovely Torbay, whilst for diners the beautiful illumination of Torquay, Paignton and Brixham and the twinkling lights of the surrounding countryside are an added joy . . .'

The actual 'opening' took place on 6 June, when Mrs Wollen (the chairman's mother) introduced 'the first visitor, the lovely Jean Kent'. After the dinner that followed 'The Queen' was toasted by the Mayor, 'Our Guests' were proposed by John Wollen and responded to by two of the guests of honour, Mr Derek Curtis Bennett, QC and Mr Leslie Mitchell. The menu—as far as the food was concerned—was in English throughout:

Dinner

* * *

Melon Cocktail in Port Wine

* * *

West Indian Turtle Broth served
with Golden Cheese Straws

* * *

Fillet of Sole 'St. Christopher'

* * *

Breast of Chicken 'Imperial Torquay'
Salad of the English Riviera

* * *

Strawberry Ice Cake 'Elizabeth'
Devonshire Dainty Delights

* * *

Empire Coffee

The list of wines begins with 'Del Pico' Fine Old Fino, followed by St Raphael; with the fish they served Riesling 1945, Grand Vin d'Alsace. There appears to have been no red wine, instead two champagnes concluded the dinner wines: Vve Clicquot-Ponsardin, Dry England 1943 and Roper Freres, Extra Dry Special Reserve 1943. (The last one is a little puzzling: one has never heard of 'Roper Freres' and in any case why would they have served one champagne after another, both of the same vintage?) Afterwards came an unnamed Armagnac, Bisquit Dubouché VSOP, or 'Liqueurs'.

It appears that at the time of its opening the sensational room was simply called 'The New Restaurant', the adjective 'aquamarine' was added later. Under whatever name—even simply as 'the dining-room'—it was a total success and has remained—with an extension added in 1961—one of the main attractions of the hotel to this day.

The dining room with its fabulous view over Torbay was opened in 1952

The following year (1953), in which the Coronation of HM Queen Elizabeth II took place, was a most successful one for The Imperial, in spite of the fact that all the euphoric action was concentrated in London, filling the capital with tourists from home and abroad. Financial success was the keynote of the report on the past year when accounts were presented at the company's AGM in July 1954. One keen observer of the hotel's progress compared the figures with those of another year in which a significant royal event took place: 1897, the time of Queen Victoria's Diamond Jubilee, when the hotel enjoyed a record annual turnover of £17,416. In the year 1953 that figure was less than the monthly average.

In his speech the Chairman (John Wollen) concluded his reference to the satisfactory results, which he regarded as exceptional, with these words: 'This was Coronation year which it is generally considered had an adverse effect on provincial hotels, but we were fortunate in having some particularly valuable conference work.' This may have been the first open reference to the fact that no hotel in the top category which is subject to the seasonal fluctuation of today's holiday habits can succeed without conference business. The fact was recognised by the Imperial management in good time and suitable provision of facilities was made in years to come.

Michael Chapman, as Managing Director, explained at the meeting his anxieties for the future in the overall picture of rising costs in every department: provisions, liquors, repairs and renewals, fuel, rates and taxes. His comments on rising salaries and wages included these prophetic observations: 'It is regrettable that the worker today does not realise that the only way to keep down prices and keep the country as a whole prosperous is to raise efficiency and production.'

The summer of 1956 saw that great nautical event, the start of the first international Sail Training Ship Race ('The Tall Ships') in Torbay, the celebrations connected with it taking place at The Imperial. The entertainments culminated on the eve of the race in a big reception in the ballroom, given by the Committee of the Sail Training Association, when the chairman, Captain John Illingworth, and his lady received about 300 guests connected with the race.

On the same evening Hugh Goodson, commodore of the Royal Dart YC (and a director of The Imperial), gave a dinner party for members of the various committees, owners of participating ships and other celebrities, including the Portuguese and Norwegian ambassadors, Admiral Pizey, Commander-in-Chief, Plymouth, the mayors of Dartmouth, Brixham and Torquay, Captain Illingworth and Mr Stavros Niarchos, owner of *Creole*.

(There was a reference to these 'happenings' at the beginning of this book; in fact . . . this is where we came in. Readers will understand and perhaps forgive the author, if from now on they find the first person, singular or plural, creeping into the narrative occasionally.)

The next important milestone in the gradual modernisation process was the creation of the Marine Sundeck Lounge, which was formally inaugurated in December 1956. Adjoining the ballroom (opened in 1935) there was a great open terrace to seaward and the new 'sundeck' made use of this space. The push-button controlled 15ft wide windows frame a breathtaking view of the bay and create the illusion of being on board an ocean liner. This feature gave us the idea of inviting a seafaring personality to perform the formal opening. After an excellent dinner the assembled guests moved into the ballroom, where curtains were drawn along one side, hiding the 'sundeck'. Captain R. J. S. Paice, master of the P & O liner *Carthage*, performed the 'launching' by opening the curtains; he was joined by another invited celebrity, film star Donald Sinden. As the curtains parted, the magnificent night

View of the hotel from the south-east, showing the 'Sundeck' Lounge, which was opened in 1956 (*J. Allan Cash*)

scene was revealed, and within seconds, the interior having been plunged into darkness, spontaneous applause by all the guests greeted a cascade of firework golden rain descending from the roof; a fine example of Michael Chapman's showmanship, performed with split-second timing!

Music for dancing and an excellent cabaret followed, and during the evening much praise was given to the revamping of the ballroom itself which was on public view for the first time. The innovations included a new sprung dance floor, with completely fresh decor and furnishings. The following night the ballroom had its first real test, being filled to capacity for the First County Ball in aid of Barnardo's Homes. 450 people supported the splendid event, who were received by Sir Peter Hoare (a director of the hotel company) and Lady Hoare,

Chairman of the Ball Committee. Led by the Lord Lieutenant of the county, Lord Fortescue, the 'top' people of Devon turned out, the High Sheriff, the Earl and Countess of Devon, Earl and Countess of Mount Edgcumbe, Earl of Morley, Lord and Lady Churston, Lord and Lady Roborough, Sir Reginald and Lady Leeds, Admiral Sir Mark Pizey (C-in-C Plymouth), MPs of several nearby constituencies, the Chief Constable of Devon, etc ... They danced till 2.30 to Billy Munn's music, and instead of the more usual buffet supper sat down in relays during the night to a full-course dinner in the restaurant. Long before the first dinner was called, the tombola stall manned by Donald Sinden was emptied—and a good time was had by all.

At the same time, some less fortunate members of the human race were not forgotten. One of the Sunday papers reported in mid-December that 'shilly-shally has robbed a Hungarian refugee family of a Christmas holiday at one of the leading hotels of Britain—the five-star Imperial at Torquay'. Three weeks earlier Michael Chapman had sent to the British Council for Aid to Refugees an invitation offering a free Christmas holiday—and had not received a reply. (This was the year of the Hungarian uprising, and many refugees, having lost everything, escaped to Britain.) Chapman was quoted by the newspaper: 'It is too late now. All our accommodation is booked. We had everything planned for a family, including presents for the children.' To which an official of the Council replied: 'We have been considering the invitation and might reach a decision on Monday ...'

In May 1957 the 'International Gastronomic Festival—Torquay' drew over 6,000 visitors to the exhibition and much favourable press comment in Britain and the rest of Europe. From small beginnings—it was started by Michael Chapman as a display of 'the culinary arts' in 1949—it had reached full maturity as a biennial event alternating with Hotelympia. The display of 29 classes and a 'table d'honneur' was mounted in the Town Hall, with the participation of distinguished entrants from several countries from the Continent.

The Imperial's involvement was most significant: Michael Chapman headed the organising council (Torquay Hotels Association and South Western Gas Board) as Chairman. William True, the chef de cuisine at The Imperial, saw to it that the hotel was well represented in the list of entries: members of his brigade, and even his apprentices, showed examples of their work, encouraged and inspired by him, gaining a large number of first prizes and other awards in appropriate classes. One of the successes which made headlines was the gold medal won by H. Belcher, one of The Imperial's sous-chefs, in the class for 'Typical

National Dishes' with his presentation of 'Boiled Beef and Carrots'. His gold medal was only one of several won by members of the Imperial staff.

Sir Alan Herbert was invited as guest of honour to the Festival and contributed magnificently to its success; members of the public flocked to the Town Hall to hear his speech at the formal opening. He illustrated the point he was making, how much gastronomy had progressed in Britain, by an anecdote centred on Hilaire Belloc, with whom he had been sailing in his cutter. During the cruise they made Portland, having fought their way through the notorious 'race'. They had several meals at the local pub and before their departure Belloc was asked by the host to write something in his visitors' book. He obliged with this couplet:

> We made a passage through St Albans Race
> And came to anchor in this bloody place.

Two important banquets were held to celebrate the Festival, both at The Imperial. The first had a menu consisting entirely of British, in fact West Country, dishes, intended no doubt for the edification of the assembled galaxy of international chefs. This was a dinner given by the Devon Branch of the International Wine & Food Society and featured Brixham lobster, shrimps and mussel pie, roast rack of Dartmoor lamb and Tamar Vale duckling in Tavistock style. We have, alas, no record of the wine list, except for a sparkling Burgundy which was served with the duck.

Sir Alan Herbert—a frequent visitor and admirer of The Imperial—was the guest speaker and during his oration he recited some verse he composed impromptu for the occasion, as a tribute to the goddess of Gastronomy:

> The sight of tables heavily dressed to dine
> The glass, the lights, the silver and the wine . . .

He went on describing the pleasures of the table and concluded:

> And, by the way, when Art has had its way,
> We fear no evils of excess next day.
> Lawyers and quacks discuss their small affairs,
> Poets, philosophers confer: who cares?
> But there's no citizen of earth, I think,
> Who has no interest in Food and Drink.

The top table at the closing banquet of the 1957 International Gastronomic Festival
(*l to r*) Mr C. H. Chester, Chairman of the South Western Gas Board; Lady Herbert;
The Mayor of Torquay, Councillor I. Joseph JP; Mr Michael Chapman, Chairman
of the Festival; The Mayoress, Mrs Joseph; Sir Alan Herbert, the principal speaker;
Mrs Chapman and Mr R. Paul (*Nicholas Horne*)

For the closing banquet, also held at The Imperial, emphasis was
laid on the international character of the event. In honour of all the
home countries of the attending visiting chefs, there was foie gras from
France, a typical German soup, Belgian sole, Scottish chicken, English
asparagus (with sauce Hollandaise no doubt), and pineapple served
with Swiss petits fours. In his speech this time, Sir Alan Herbert
expressed the hope that the proper emphasis had been given to the
international aspect of friendship by the Festival. Compared to other
kinds of international meetings, concerned with disarmament and
world peace, he felt much more hopeful about international co-
operation and harmony in the catering industry. 'Its arts are common
to mankind,' he said, 'whereas the H-bomb is an acquired taste ...'

There was another colourful event in Torquay only a few weeks later, in the third week of June, involving The Imperial. This was an elaborately planned charity event in aid of the National Institute for the Deaf, organised by Mrs Olga Noble-Mathews (a leading charity organiser); it comprised yacht racing, a concours d'elegance for cars, music, dancing, sideshows and barbecues; it was tagged by one of the glossy magazines a 'Torquay Cavalcade'. The starting point for the cavalcade was in London, where the Lord Mayor, Sir Cullum Welch, formally dispatched a convoy of cars on the road to Torquay. Led by Sheila Van Damm, the drivers and passengers included many stage, film and TV personalities and were welcomed on arival in Torquay by the Mayor and Mayoress, Mr and Mrs A. L. Goodrich.

On the next day a sailing race was given by the Royal Torbay Yacht Club for the Silent World Cup, presented by Mr A. E. Johnson, followed by the splendid concours d'elegance of beautifully turned out cars: big cars, small cars, old cars, new cars ... A giant open-air

Some of the distinguished participants in the events organised in aid of the National Institute for the Deaf in June 1957 at The Imperial (*top row, l to r*) Joe Henderson, Frances Day, Donald Healey, Mrs Olga Noble-Matthews (the organiser), Tommy Sampson, Jeanne Heal, F. Mullally; (*bottom row*) Mary Malcolm, Sheila Van Damm, Tony Britten, Elizabeth Welch (*Barrow's Photo Service*)

One of the new 'studio' rooms opened in 1958 (*Nicholas Horne*)

barbecue attracted a large crowd, who ardently pursued the attending celebrities for their autographs. The festivities terminated and culminated in a Champagne Supper Dance and Cabaret at The Imperial (where else?), patronised by the Earl and Countess of Harewood, Earl and Countess of Devon, Viscount Soulbury, Lady Patricia Lennox-Boyd, Lord and Lady Roborough and many other members of the 'élite'. The cabaret performers were Frances Day, Tony Britton, Mary Malcolm, Pete Murray, Sheila Van Damm, Joe Henderson, Elizabeth Welch, the West Indian Calypso Group and the Moonrakers Skiffle Group of the RNAS.

The modernisation and development of the old hotel building continued with sustained vigour and enterprise. The next phase of this almost never-ending process was the construction of eighteen new studio rooms on two floors overlooking the garden and the sea, below the ground-floor level (underneath the new dining-room opened in 1952). These apartments, fourteen doubles and four singles, were built within an existing, original colonnade at the top of a slope. The rooms,

The praline ice 'Tree of Friendship' being served during a banquet of the International Gastronomic Festival, 1959

which could almost be regarded as suites, comprise a large 'dayroom', from which the sleeping area can be curtained off during the daytime, fully tiled bathroom, lobby and in some cases separate dressing-room. They all have a private sun balcony with huge plate-glass windows and doors overlooking the sea, and on the lower level have direct access to the gardens. The decor is modern, with built-in furniture designed to fit each apartment.

By the summer of 1958 the new 'terrace rooms' were completed and ready for occupation, the opening ceremony being performed on 18 July by F. J. Errol, MP, Parliamentary Secretary to the Board of Trade (who was later to become Lord Errol) and J. G. Bridges, OBE, the Director General of the British Travel Association (the future British Tourist Authority). These two gentlemen were also the first occupiers of the new rooms.

The principle of large windows and private balconies for each room was to be extended gradually to the whole seafront facade of the hotel, and so these rooms were a foretaste of things to come.

The following year (1959) saw another highly successful International Gastronomic Festival, in which The Imperial again took the leading part. Lady Lewisham (the future Lady Dartmouth and now Lady Spencer, step-mother of The Princess of Wales) was the official opener of the show, and she was also one of the speakers at the Wine & Food Society dinner at The Imperial in the evening; the other one was André Simon CBE, the society's octogenarian President. At the closing banquet two nights later the Rt Hon Ernest Marples was the principal speaker.

It was a perfect summer afternoon for the ceremonial opening of the new outdoor swimming pool on 25 July. There was a water-ballet and a demonstration swim by a young lady swimming champion, and cocktails were served on the pool's mosaic terraces. The formal opening with a suitable brief address was again performed by F. J. Errol, who surprised the assembled VIPs and other guests by swiftly disrobing after his speech and being the first to dive in, with great panache.

These were the years of continuous expansion and modernisation. Several phases of the plans prepared by Michael Chapman and the hotel's architects, Guise Davies & Upfold of London, followed each other in quick succession. During the extended period some building

The outdoor swimming pool, in its lovely clifftop setting, was opened in the summer of 1959 (*J. Allan Cash*)

work was in progress all the time, but miraculously the business of the hotel went on undisturbed, and guests suffered no inconvenience or discomfort.

An important milestone was marked in June 1961 by the opening of the new extension of the dining room, which added a further 2,500 sq ft of floor space. At the same time two floors of further luxury studio rooms had been completed below. The complete new wing was formally declared open by the Duke of Richmond and Gordon, in his capacity as President of the British Travel & Holidays Association. He started his speech by saying that he had opened many buildings, offices and even a football ground in Scotland, but never had he enjoyed an opening as much as this one. He paid tribute to Michael Chapman and his staff on the service and atmosphere of The Imperial: 'It is not the slightest use having a magnificent building if what goes on inside it is no good—if the service is bad. Let the managing director and the board be praised for the *esprit d'Imperial*, which is a marvellous thing in this hotel. There is a spirit here which you do not find in many places.' He described Michael Chapman as a 'perfectionist'.

The improvements completed so far were only the beginnings of the great scheme with which The Imperial had entered the 1960s. The

The 'new face' of The Imperial was completed (*Nicholas Horne*)

whole scheme—originally estimated to cost £250,000, but it must have cost much more before it was completed—involved a great deal more. It was considered by Michael Chapman and his board that it was essential to carry out the work if The Imperial 'was to maintain its position as one of the leading hotels in Europe'. They declared in 1960: 'Within the next four years the exterior—and much of the interior— will be completely renovated and the world-famous hotel with its commanding views of Torbay will be as modern and charmingly functional as any hotel in this country. The new wing will accommodate thirty new bedrooms, all with bathrooms and balconies and all facing the sea.'

The piecemeal development of the past—the only way possible without serious disruption—had led to The Imperial showing several forms and styles of architecture, the original old, Victorian 'Italianate' decorative masonry being in sharp contrast with the style of the new dining-room and the already completed bedroom wings. This was to be remedied to the full; as the architects put it succinctly, 'the old hotel will have the appearance of the very latest of modern luxury hotels'.

1961 also saw the beginning of another important innovation: in the autumn the first of The Imperial's international gastronomic weekends took place—a subject which calls for a separate chapter.

8
A Hundred Years
of Gastronomy

8

The Imperial's gastronomic tradition can be traced back to the time when Napoleon III stayed there and greatly enjoyed the cooking. Nor has gastronomy been neglected in more recent times, under Michael Chapman's regime of over forty years. For he has a full understanding of the paramount importance of good food and drink, although he is a man of frugal personal tastes. We have seen that when the international Gastronomic Festival of Torquay was started, to become a regular biennial event, he was the prime mover and thus his hotel became known as a gastronomic haven in Britain, even in the eyes of visiting professionals from the Continent.

By the beginning of the 1960s, with such a background, Michael Chapman's leadership and the exceptional talents of his chef at the time, William True, the time was ripe for something more far-reaching, something that would give widespread pleasure in the field of gastronomy to existing and future clients of the hotel.

In my extensive travels throughout Europe I could not help noticing how much the indigenous cooking of a country or region was apt to lose its original, intrinsic character and integrity when transplanted into alien soil. One could not fail to see the vast difference between a well-prepared dish, or a whole meal, in a good restaurant abroad and the product of a so-called French, Italian or other ethnic restaurant in London or, say, New York. There were also clear signs to be noted everywhere of a growing interest in the cuisines of other regions and countries. Gastronomic festivals, 'weeks', or just dinners were being offered everywhere, presenting the work of visiting chefs and restaurateurs. Famous among such events at the time were the regular seasons of 'Semaines Gastronomiques' at Aix-en-Provence, whole weeks during which a visiting chef's specialities could be ordered à la carte, culminating in a *diner de gala*. There were also the so called 'Gastronomic Weekends' held during the winters at the Kursaal in Ostend. Here, different famous chefs were invited to present a dinner on a Saturday night for as many as 500 guests, many of whom came long distances. The charge included the stay in a hotel for the night and breakfast—of course they were expected to visit the gaming rooms after dinner.

When I suggested to Michael Chapman that we should introduce our own version of similar gastronomic events, it became clear to both of us that it should be more complete and comprehensive than had been tried elsewhere. From the very beginning we established a basic formula which has proved successful. Our weekends start on Friday afternoon and end on Monday morning; they include, apart from breakfasts, five gastronomic meals: three dinners and two lunches.

For the first series of such weekends in 1961–2 we invited first-class restaurants, but as this was our first experiment we thought it wiser not to try to be too ambitious, so they were not of the exalted (Michelin three star) rank, just good, genuine and personally known to us. A typical example was the visiting establishment at our first Gastronomic Weekend, the Grand Hotel Bardet et Regina, of Le Mont Dore, which had a Michelin star at the time and which I had visited—M Louis Virot, the chef-patron, was known to me personally, and he brought with him his assistant chef, M Paul Weiss.

As to the programme, we moved warily at first. We could not be absolutely sure if the guests—between forty and fifty booked for the first weekend—would enjoy the 'foreign' cooking at every meal. Nor was it certain that the collaboration of the visiting chefs with our own and his brigade would be an unreservedly happy one. For these two reasons during the first two or three weekends the menus offered an alternative choice of The Imperial's own specialities, course by course. The Saturday's *diner de gala* had the only fixed menu: an Auvergnat menu and an historic occasion:

Le Potage Bisque d'Ecrevisses
* * *
La Truite Farcie 'Reine Margot'
* * *
Le Coq au Vin d'Auvergne
* * *
La Mousseline de Pommes Mont-Dore
* * *
Les fromages des Burons
* * *
La Tarte des Reinettes Feuilletée

The white wine was a Saint-Pourcain-sur-Sioule 1959, the nearest thing to a local wine in the Auvergne, and this was followed by a superb Gevrey Chambertin, Clos de la Justice 1953 with the main course. It was said at the time, with some astonishment, that twelve bottles of wine were poured into the chicken dish; we only hope that it was not the precious Gevrey Chambertin!

By contrast, this was the choice put on by William True and his brigade as an alternative, at lunchtime: Brixham Shrimp, Lobster and Mushroom Flan, Soufflé Quenelles of Salmon, Roast Scotch Pheasant, Braised Spiced Sugared Ham with a Glazed Peach and Pineapple Garnish; the vegetables were most attractively described—Chestnut-flavoured Brussels Sprouts, Oven-baked Potato Pancake, Buttered Sugared Garden Peas and Thyme-flavoured Roast Potatoes. No wonder that the late Philip Harben—television cook at the time—when reporting one of the earliest weekends in *Woman's Own*, wrote: 'The management have not given the resident English kitchen brigade the weekend off—on the contrary! . . . the thing has developed into a sort of culinary Test Match. At the moment, with three meals to go, it's just about even Steven . . . result next week.'

The precaution of offering the English alternative quickly proved unnecessary, for the guests really wanted the imported cuisine and the chefs worked together in the greatest amity. During those few days they invariably become firm friends, respecting each other's professional skill, and they will freely admit that they have something to learn from each other. Many of the guests thought it distinctly hilarious at first when they saw the two chefs embracing and kissing each other on both cheeks in public after the farewell dinner on Sunday night, but it wasn't long before they accepted it as a sincere expression of friendship and respect for each other. The 'kissing' has never stopped since that first weekend—it still happens every time.

The first series (1961–2) consisted of four weekends, and the news of the idea soon got around, through the favourable press comments and word-of-mouth recommendations; the numbers of guests attending grew and grew. In the second, third and fourth years there were still four weekends per season, but from 1965 it was possible to increase the number, first to five and soon to six, which became the usual number.

From the early days the main features of the programme for each weekend crystallised, so that regular attenders know exactly what to expect. Invariably there is a champagne or similar reception before dinner each night, dancing in the ballroom and later in the nightclub afterwards. There is an excursion to a Devon beauty spot on Saturday

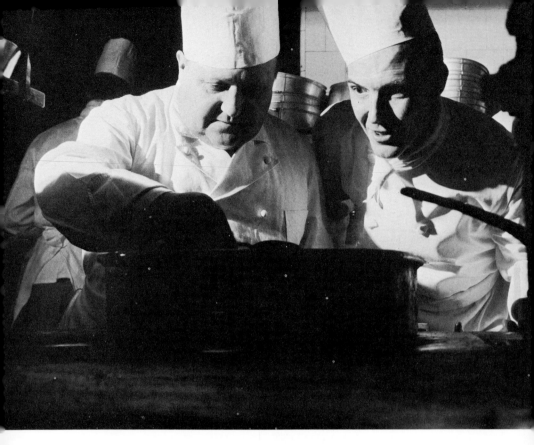

In the kitchen during one of the early Gastronomic Weekends: (*left*) M Emile Tingaud, famous chef-patron of the Auberge de Condé, La Ferté-sous-Jouarre with William True, then Head Chef of The Imperial (*Falcon Stuart/Tom Hustler Studios*)

morning, invariably with a stop for a drink at some ancient hostelry, a cookery demonstration by the visiting chefs in the afternoon, a special wine-tasting on Sunday morning and a film show in the afternoon. For each weekend a particular wine shipper or merchant is chosen to supply all the wines, carefully selected to match the food at the dinners and lunches, and also to put on the tasting.

It was clear that the weekends had 'taken off' from the start; they offered exceptional value to the guests who did not have to put their hands in their pockets at all, as everything was (and still is) included in the charges; it is of some interest that in 1961–2 the full, inclusive charges ranged from 16 guineas (£16.80) to 21 guineas (£22.05) per person.

Another feature that distinguishes these weekends is that through-out guests have changed for dinner every night, and nobody has ever found it too much trouble to put on a dinner jacket—or a long or short evening dress. On the contrary, 'dressing' for dinner, seems to add to the enjoyment.

With the exception of 'Le Panier d'Or' of Bruges, all the visiting restaurants were French during the early years. By the beginning of the third season of the international events, the hotel was full for the weekend, which happened to be another French one, featuring 'En Plein Ciel' the restaurant of the Eiffel Tower in Paris, run by André Pignarre, one of the leading gourmet personalities of the French capital and a great showman. He put on an excellent show, which culminated with the presentation at the end of the gala dinner, to special suitable musical accompaniment, of several replicas of the Eiffel Tower—in ice cream. This was only one of a number of his trump cards. On the same evening, as a complete surprise to all concerned, M Georges Libersart, Minister Plenipotentiary, Com-mercial Counsellor at the French Embassy in London, who was present with Madame as a special guest, got up to make an amusing speech after dinner. He concluded by announcing that Michael Chapman had been awarded a decoration by the French government in recognition of his efforts to promote French cuisine and products. There and then, he presented him with the cross of the Chevalier du Merite Agricole. It was a fairly safe guess that the organising of the Gastronomic Weekends had something to do with the award; M Libersart himself had attended on a previous occasion, during the preceding season.

Following this highly successful weekend, early in 1964, members of The Imperial's kitchen brigade won several prizes in the Salon Culinaire against stiff competition at Hotelympia in London.

The fame of the Gastronomic Weekends was spreading not only in Britain—witness the growing number of guests, now often filling the hotel—but also on the other side of the Channel. The willing cooperation of the French official tourist bodies and French Railways brought a large folkdance group to The Imperial to add colour and zest to the Alsace Weekend in January 1964. They did just that as the girls in bright dresses and young men with festive ribbons trailing from their hats wound their way through the tables, dancing to the tune of accordions and flutes. They were soon intermingled with the tall white-hatted chefs, who had come into the room to receive the praise and acclamation of the guests. Local colour for the Swiss Weekend which closed the 1963-4 season was provided by similar national touches—these included a competition for blowing a gigantic alpenhorn and another for the best yodeller.

The following season saw the first Italian Weekend (February 1965), for which we obtained the participation of the 'Restaurant Fini', which at that time was regarded by experts as the finest in the whole country, and was in the gastronomically superb region of Emilia. Not only Parma ham but several other unique charcuterie products come from there, such as the famous 'zampone', a sausage of exquisite, delicate flavour in the shape of a pig's leg. Dr Giorgio Fini, our guest patron, was determined to include some zampone in the weekend's menus, and some unexpected delay was caused by HM Customs at Heathrow, when some of these delicacies were flown over. They were put on a train in London, to be picked up by the hotel at Torquay station, just in time for the weekend. I remember that when they failed to arrive, the hotel's head chef himself, the great William True, got into his car and drove many miles to another railway station, where the zampone was reported to have turned up in error.

At the beginning of 1965 it was announced by the three motoring organisations that only three hotels outside London, in the whole of the United Kingdom, were worthy of five-star classification: Gleneagles, The Carlton, Bournemouth and The Imperial, Torquay. It was interesting to note that at that time the minimum required for this grade was that 75 per cent of the bedrooms should have private baths, whereas The Imperial had a good hundred! The loss of stars by seven other out-of-London hotels created an outcry countrywide, but of course the number of bathrooms was not the only criterion.

The 1965 Gastronomic Weekend season ended in March with a visit of the 'Troisgros' restaurant from Roanne; it had a star for its cuisine in the Guide Michelin, and since that time has become one of France's very top rank restaurants, with three well-deserved stars.

Meanwhile The Imperial's own unaided efforts in the art of cooking gained full recognition. A West Country Weekend organised for the International Wine & Food Society for its members from all parts of the country, was a great success, and resulting from a visit by a leading Dutch restaurateur to the Imperial the hotel was invited to send a team of chefs to Amsterdam, during a British Week to be held there. Led by William True, the team were to present a week of British menus at the 'Havenrestaurant'; the dishes chosen were to be based on West Country specialities, similar to those which were so highly praised by members of the Wine & Food Society.

The International Gastronomic Festival brought more successes for The Imperial that year. There was a Festival Banquet at The Imperial, given by the Mayor and Corporation of Torquay in association with the Torquay Hotels Association and the Council of the International Gastronomic Festival for the delegates attending the 1965 Congress of FIPREGA (Federation Internationale de la Presse Gastronomique et Vinicole), which was organised by myself as the British Vice-President of the Federation. The eighty or so delegates had come down to Torquay to see the Festival and stayed the night at The Imperial, where they were welcomed by the Mayor during the splendid banquet, consisting entirely of British food.

Lord Boyd of Merton, prominent parliamentarian and former Colonial Secretary, was the principal guest speaker at the closing banquet of the Festival. He recalled his wartime experiences, when as Commander Lennox-Boyd, RNVR, in a fast torpedo boat he would flash across Torbay from Brixham, heading for Torquay. It served the double purpose of carrying out speed trials, and of conveying the good-food-hungry officer towards The Imperial, where he was sure to find satisfaction through the kind offices of his old friend, Michael Chapman . . .

Here is the menu for the FIPREGA banquet.

Medaillons of Creamed Dart Salmon
Festival Garnish
* * *
Cornish Chicken Broth
Savoury Cheese Triangles
* * *
Torbay Sole St. Michael's Mount
* * *
Larded Fillet of Red Devon Beef
English Riviera Garnish
Cottage Cheese Potato Cake
Purple Sprouting Broccoli, Egg Sauce
* * *
Devonshire Cream Ice Cake
Exevale Morello Cherries flamed in Plymouth Sloe Gin
* * *
Imperial Sweetmeats

For the closing banquet, the menu was as follows.

Devon Beef Broth
Golden Cheese Wafers

* * *

Turbot in Gastronomic Cloak

* * *

Spiced Chicken in Melon
Cornish Vegetable Garnish
Oriental Potato Cake

* * *

Lemon Sherbert

* * *

Saddle of milk-fed Veal
Braised Fennel
Creamed Spinach Tartlets
Curly Endive Salad

* * *

Maraschino Soufflé

* * *

Sweetmeats and Fondant Creams

Before the commencement of the 1965–6 season Michael Chapman revealed the plans for forming the Imperial Gourmet Club, 'arising out of the series of Gastronomic Weekends for which the hotel has now achieved an international reputation'. Reporting this, the *Herald Express* continued, quoting myself: 'An invisible link has been forged during these occasions, not only among the many guests who had attended, but also between them and the visiting chefs and restaurateurs. To strengthen these links it is intended to form the Imperial Gourmet Club to unite those who attend the gastronomic weekends. The restaurateurs who have participated so far, and those who will attend in the future, will be asked to join this circle, and so a chain will emerge of some of the finest gourmet hotels and restaurants of the Continent in alliance with The Imperial and its clients. Our members will receive a very special welcome whenever they visit one of the allied establishments and it is also hoped that they will also enjoy certain privileges, both at The Imperial and the others.'

The Gourmet Club reunion has become a regular feature of the weekend's programme these days, and our members are issued with a 'passport' to be presented for identification when visiting the member establishments.

By the time the fifth season (1965–6) was due to begin the weekends had 'arrived' and almost every time the hotel was completely filled. The first was another West Country Weekend, organised in partnership with the Wine & Food Society; this included a visit for luncheon in the ancient cellars of a famous firm of Plymouth wine merchants. Next came the Basque Weekend with M Pierre Laporte's 'Café de Paris' of Biarritz.

The next weekend, in January 1966, could be regarded as a historic event, if only for the reason that it could never be repeated. It was christened the 'France Afloat' Weekend, and the chefs of the famous transatlantic liner, the lovely *France*, presented their specialities; one of the desserts was served as a model of the great ship, made of ice cream. Then came a Normandy Weekend with M Maurice Lalonde—Hotel de la Marine, Caudebec-en-Caux. The champagne happened to be Pol Roger, and the delightful lady of that name was there in person. This inspired one of the writers present to tell a little story when reporting the weekend: 'Puns department (French section): I was about to introduce somebody to Mme. Pol Roger. "Do you know her?" I asked. "No," he said, "but I once met her Mumm."' (With the author's abject apologies.)

A highly successful season closed with a Champagne Weekend, featuring the 'Royal Champagne' of Champillon, near Epernay, which was run for many years by the fabulous character M Desvignes.

The Gastronomic Weekends gained a special significance in their 1966–7 season which coincided with The Imperial's Centenary. The hotel having first opened in November 1866, the weekend of 11 to 14 November 1966 was designated for the celebration. Thanks to the imagination and showmanship of Michael Chapman and William True, it was much more than just a fine weekend, more a veritable gastronomic *tour de force*. In spite of the fact that hardly any of the hotel's records had survived the last war, they managed to present five meals, each representing a different period of those hundred years.

Friday's opening dinner was in the late Edwardian style, c1910. The menu, which is shown on the following page, was based on a Mayoral Banquet served at The Imperial in 1910.

Dinner

* * *

Cornets de Saumon Fumé au Caviar

* * *

Consommé Royale

* * *

Délices de Sole Edouard VII

* * *

Caneton à la Bigarade

Petis Pois à la Menthe

Endives Braisées au Madère

Pommes Marquise

* * *

Bombe Imperiale

* * *

Cerises Flambées au Cognac

* * *

Petits Fours

* * *

Pailles au Parmesan

* * *

Café

Wines

* * *

Reception

Champagne Bollinger, Cuvée Speciale

* * *

Dinner

Pouilly Blanc Fumé 1964

Chaville Selection

Clos-de-Vougeot 1961

Geisweiler & Fils

Château Coutet 1961

Fine Champagne Cognac, Delamain

Dow's Boardroom Tawny

Crème de Menthe, Cusenier

The toast 'Our Guests and Friends in the Hotel and Wine Trade' was given by the late Travers Mooyaart, a director of the hotel company and a witty speaker, and the responses by Mr Vernon Duker, Chairman of the Torquay Hotels Association, and Mr Anthony Leschallas, director of Mentzendorff & Co, the wine shippers, respectively. Saturday's luncheon was in the late Victorian style of 1890, and it was indicated that the same menu at the time would have cost 3s (15p)—presumably not including the wines.

LUNCHEON 1890

* * *

Hors d'Oeuvres Riches

* * *

Carré de Pré-salé Rôti
Primeurs de Cornouailles
Pommes Boulangère

* * *

Savarin Victoria
Pêches Crème Double

* * *

Fromages d'Angleterre: Crème – Stilton – Cheddar

* * *

Café

The wines were only two: Bernkasteler Herrenberg 1964 and Beaune St Vincent 1962; at the end there was Dow's Old Vintage Character Port and Cusenier VSOP Brandy.

The climax of the celebrations, the Centenary Banquet, was attended by about 400 guests, who were served by waiters wearing Victorian sideburns in the beautifully decorated, flower-decked dining-room. The menu which is shown on the following page, closely followed that of the inaugural dinner held in November 1866.

During the reception two kinds of sherry were offered: Findlater's Tia Lola, Fino Delicado, and Findlater's Cecilia, Dry Amontillado. With dinner came Batard Montrachet 1962, Château Ausone 1957 (le 1er cru St Emilion) and magnums of Bollinger 1959, Extra Quality; Delamain Fine Champagne Cognac and Cusenier's Apricot Brandy concluded the list.

DINNER 1866

* * *

HORS D'OEUVRES
Foie Gras de Strasbourg à la Gelée de Porto

* * *

POTAGE
Consommé à l'Imperial

* * *

POISSON
Délice de Turbot à la Reine

* * *

ENTRÉE
Selle de Chevreuil Grand Veneur
Choufleur à la Polonaise
Pommes Mousseline

* * *

SORBET
Bollinger Granité aux Mandarines

* * *

ROTI
Poulet de Grain au Cresson
Pommes Pailles
Salade à la Perigord

* * *

ENTREMET
Bombe Nesselrode
Douceurs des Dames
Café

'The Queen' was proposed by the Mayor of Torquay, Alderman L. S. W. Howard, JP, and the main speech of the evening, in the form of the toast 'The Imperial, Torquay', was given by the guest of honour, Lord Shawcross, President of the British Hotels Association. He congratulated The Imperial on its hundredth anniversary and on the job it was doing, as one of Europe's premier hotels, earning badly needed foreign exchange. 'We must earn as much from abroad as we spend overseas and the hotel industry, and this hotel in particular, is making a very important contribution.' From this point he launched an eloquent attack on the government of the day, severely criticising them for not giving sufficient, much-needed assistance to the hotel and tourist industries. His fighting speech was widely reported.

The response to it first came from John Wollen, Chairman of the hotel company, who traced the history of The Imperial over the past hundred years. 'But we are not old or out-dated', he emphasised, 'The Imperial of the 1960s is a hotel of today, but with a century of goodwill and experience behind it.' The last speaker, Mr Hugh Goodson, Vice Chairman of the board, told the gathering that he looked upon The Imperial as 'almost a national institution'.

Special awards were presented to several long-serving members of the hotel staff by the Chairman; Harry Cocks, a waiter with 51 years of service led the seniority stakes. Others included Mrs Phil Kitley-Carter, hostess (24 years), G. Taylor, head porter (24 years), T. Moore, head engineer (21 years), W. Scobie, hall porter (21 years), Dennis Eldergill, head barman (22 years) and several others. It was calculated at the time that there were altogether 15 people with more than 20 years service and 30 with over 10 years: between them, these 45 people totalled 750 years of service. There was also a special presentation to William True, the chef de cuisine, who was given an inscribed silver tankard amid lively applause.

As a complete surprise to the banquet guests, at the end of the festive proceedings all the lights went out to reveal a spectacular firework display in the grounds. Dancing in the ballroom to the music of Billy Munn and his orchestra and later in the Commodore Night Club completed the celebrations; and so The Imperial was launched for its second century . . .

Sunday's luncheon was on slightly simpler lines. It was dated 1935 (George V style) and the menu was in French:

Crèpe Marinière St. George

* * *

Côte de Veau Cordon Bleu
Epinards Mornay – Pommes Parisienne

* * *

Tarte à la Reine
Fromages de Normandie: Demi-sel – Camembert – Marcellin

Wines
Pouilly Fuissé 1964
Gevrey Chambertin 1961
Imperial Vintage Character Port
Fine Maison VSOP

The Farewell Dinner on Sunday night brought us back to 1966, and the menu was in English following the post-war Imperial tradition:

A 1966 DINNER

* * *

Dorset Quail Paté

* * *

Torbay Lobster in Brandy Cream

* * *

Fillet of Devon Beef, Tarragon Sauce
Buttered Runner Beans
Almond Rolled Potatoes

* * *

Pineapple Sherbet

* * *

Roast Moorland Pheasant, Savoury Toastlet
Rich Game Sauce, Lettuce Hearts, Wine Dressing

* * *

Centenary Soufflé
Imperial Sweetmeats

* * *

Coffee

At the reception, Bollinger Special Cuvée was served; the wines during dinner were Puligny Montrachet 1962, Château Montrose 1959 and Château Climens 1962.

Michael Chapman (Manager from 1939 and Managing Director from 1943) gave a toast this time to 'Our Visitors and The British Press', showing his appreciation of the contribution both those categories make to The Imperial's success. Derek Young, the distinguished writer and journalist, editor of the BTA's magazine *In Britain* and a great admirer of the hotel, responded in glowing terms.

After the exceptional Centenary celebration the progression of the Gastronomic Weekends continued. Distinguished visitors followed each other during the rest of the season (1966–7): the three-star (Michelin) 'Ousteau de Beaumanière' from Provence, Kempinski of West Berlin, 'Ristorante Apicio' from Rome and Kai Olsen's hotel from Vejle in Denmark extended gastronomic horizons. It was after the end of this season, in April 1967, that William True decided that he wanted to conquer fresh fields and left to take another job in charge of the kitchens of a new restaurant in Toronto. He had been at The Imperial for fifteen years.

The Gastronomic Weekends were 'going from strength to strength' as one noted wine and food writer put it. The high standards in The Imperial's kitchens were maintained under the new head chef, J. Elvin, who had followed True. His fish and egg chef, twenty-six-year-old Michael Hawke, won a gold medal for the second time running at Hotelympia in January 1968: his entry comprised a sweet omelette, a savoury omelette with Torbay seafood and an original dish based on hard-boiled eggs and avocado pear.

Storm-clouds blanketed the Torquay skies for a short time in February 1968 when the rivalry between two powerful trade unions caused problems for some of the hotels in the town, and willy-nilly The Imperial was affected. The Transport & General Workers Union was eager to gain ground in the hotels, following a dispute in one of them the previous summer. The Imperial had hoped not to be affected by this action at all, for those staff members who belonged to a union were members of the Municipal & General Workers. When pickets were posted outside The Imperial—and several other hotels—trying to prevent supplies being delivered, including oil used for heating, the situation became threatening and hit the headlines in the regional and national press. The hotel management sought the advice of a London barrister who specialised in trade-union law.

Without delay a warning was sent to the TGWU, as required by the law, and when this was ignored, an application for an interim injunction to the High Court met with success and the pickets were withdrawn at once. When the case came up for trial, the injunction was confirmed and The Imperial was awarded £15,000 damages and costs. Later the Court of Appeal confirmed the judgement, and the union decided not to make a further appeal to the House of Lords. It should be noted that the law has been changed since.

Even gastronomic achievements don't always go unrecognised. One such exception came to Michael Chapman by the hand of the Grand Old Man of Gastronomy in the United Kingdom, the US and many other countries, the late André Simon, CBE, President of the International Wine & Food Society. It was at a dinner at the Savoy in London celebrating his ninety-first birthday that he personally presented Michael Chapman, in the presence of over 100 members, with the society's medal; it was the first time a British hotelier was so honoured. The citation was: 'The president and members of the management committee of the Int. Wine & Food Society are aware of the exceptionally constant high standard of cuisine and service which has made The Imperial Hotel, Torquay famous among gastronomes. This does Mr. Chapman the greatest possible credit. Therefore they have awarded him the society's medal as a token of their appreciation of his valuable services to the cause of gastronomy.' (It must be remarked that the medal was at that time the only award of the society. It was some years later that 'grades' of gold, silver and bronze were introduced.)

The Gastronomic Weekends each brought new interest, ideas and colours to an ever-growing number of guests. New countries took part as well as new regions, and Spain, Hungary and Sweden joined the ranks of the old favourites. The first Swedish Weekend will remain for a long time in my memory, for the agonies I suffered in connection with the supply of—never guess—reindeer meat. Through the years we had learned a great deal about the problems that might arise over the import of rare ingredients, sometimes unobtainable in Britain. Experience has taught us to avoid doing so whenever possible. It was therefore against my better judgement and with great reluctance that I accepted the rather insistent suggestion of our Stockholm collaborator in the first Swedish Weekend that reindeer should be included in one of the menus. 'It will be so easy to send some over,' they assured me. Well it was not that easy. The documentation was formidable. I spent considerable time obtaining the various permits and certificates from HM Customs, the Ministry of Ag & Fish and the veterinary authorities of both countries. At last all was in order and the meat was on the way in a refrigerated lorry. I gave instructions that should the lorry not be able to deliver in Torquay, the meat should be unloaded at a certain cold store in London.

One fine morning I had a phone call from a kind customs officer I got to know during the preliminaries, from Dover, telling me with joy that our meat had just passed through in the lorry. Alas, it disappeared after that ... it had not been delivered at either place. This was desperate. I rang my friend at the Customs in Dover the next day, just to check. He informed me that the vehicle in question had passed through, empty. It took much cabling and telephoning to Sweden before we discovered that the reindeer meat had been delivered in London, but at a totally different warehouse. In the end we had just enough time to collect it on the day it was wanted; it thawed out while being driven to Torquay. When cooked, I found little to commend it ... must be more careful next time, I decided.

The Wine & Food Society, founded by André Simon in 1933 in London, had about 7,500 members by 1969, of whom about a third were British, a third American and a third spread over the rest of the world. A year or two earlier the word International was added to its name, and the First Convention was held in Chicago in 1967. The Second Convention took place in England from 9 to 13 October 1969, and it was a great honour for The Imperial that most of the time was spent there.

The Convention opened with a fine champagne reception and supper at the Café Royal, and the following morning (Friday) a special train, consisting of all-Pullman dining coaches, took the 300 or so delegates to Torquay. They had champagne as an aperitif and an excellent lunch on the way. Nearly all were accommodated in the hotel, which by this time had just about the required capacity. The President of the Society, in his ninety-third year, attended and was feted by the delegates—the majority of whom came from the US— every time he entered the dining-room or elsewhere. The event was covered by BBC television; James Burke reported in detail—including some interviews with the President and myself, in my capacity as Convention director.

There was a great deal of intricate organisation involved, not only to ensure smooth running but also to give every delegate the feeling of being personally looked after and cosseted in the lap of luxury. For example, all the luggage was distributed to the rooms after it had been brought in special vehicles from the railway station, to be found by each individual on arrival. To make this possible they were invited to partake in the 'Devonshire Tea' on arrival, before going to their room. Seating at all the meals was carefully worked out and changed around each time to enable people to have different contacts and make more friends. On the opening night after a champagne reception (Pommery & Greno, the President's favourite marque) there was a 'Torbay Seafood Dinner' accompanied by a Grand Cru Chablis, a Corton-Charlemagne, a Montrachet and finally a Hattenheimer Rothenburg Riesling Beerenauslese (with the dessert), all of a single year, 1966.

After the formalities of the official opening by the President, who also presented several of the Society's medals next morning, delegates adjourned from the hotel's ballroom to the Marine Spa—at the bottom of the hill—within a short walk, for a grand tasting of German wines conducted by Fritz Hallgarten. (The delightful early Victorian Marine Spa was demolished later, making way for the hideous monstrosity called 'Coral Island'. The Imperial's own superb conference hall, the Astra Room, had not been built yet, hence the use of outside premises.)

There was a Game Lunch to follow, comprising Dorset quail, Dartmoor venison (soup) and Exmoor pheasant, with a Sancerre 1968 and a rare and fine Châteauneuf-du Pape 1964, ending with a 1947 Tuke-Holdsworth Port.

For those intrepid enough an excursion was laid on during the afternoon to Compton Castle (where the colonisation of America is said to have been planned by Sir Walter Raleigh and Sir Humphrey Gilbert, whose descendants still live there) and later, after tea, films of the 'Master Chefs' (sponsored by the Society) were shown. After another champagne reception (Laurent-Perrier this time) there was an 'Imperial West Country Dinner':

Cornish Beef and Chicken Broth

* * *

Fillet of Halibut St. Michael's Mount

* * *

Roast Larded Fillet of Beef in Pastry
Rich Wine Sauce, Cornish Vegetable Platter
Devonshire Potato Cake

* * *

Cheddar Cheese Soufflé

* * *

Devon Apple Imperial 'Wine & Food' Parfait

* * *

Mints and Sweetmeats

* * *

Coffee

The wines were out of this world: a La Riva Solera 1840 sherry with the soup, Château Laville-Haut-Brion 1964 (white) with the fish, followed by two extremely rare clarets Château Mouton Baron-Philippe 1945 (in magnums), Château Mouton-Rothschild 1934 (magnums) ending with the great sauternes, Château d'Yquem 1949.

The great clarets were the result of years of search and planning by the Society's Wine Committee, and had been purchased well ahead for just such an occasion. They needed careful handling and cellaring too, and I had arranged to have them sent to the hotel about three months in advance so as to give them a chance of a good rest. I remember discussing this with Michael Chapman sometime during the preceding summer. We found there was no room in the hotel's wine cellar and someone suggested a disused room in the basement of the West Wing (the erstwhile Villa Marina of long ago). The two of us went down to this room and had it unlocked, only to find, stacked from floor to ceiling . . . hundreds of forgotten chamberpots. I don't know what happened to those, but the room was cleared and made the perfect cellar for the priceless, treasured wines.

On Sunday morning there were three parallel tastings of Australian, Californian and South African wines at the Marine Spa, an 'Italian' lunch at the hotel, followed by a general discussion of the Assembly in the ballroom and after tea a draw, in which the first prize was a double magnum of Château Lafite 1865 (pre-phylloxera). The evening began with a tasting of eighteen marques of vintage champagne; they ranged in alphabetical order from Bollinger to Veuve-Clicquot, and continued with a 'French Banquet':

Ballotine de Foie de Caneton
* * *
Consommé St. Hubert
* * *
Feuilleté d'Homard, Sauce Normande
* * *
Côte de Veau Forestière
* * *
Pommes Dauphine
* * *
Fromages de France
* * *
Soufflé Glacé des Liqueurs
* * *
Mignardises des Dames
* * *
Café

The wines ranged from a simple Muscadet, Château de la Galissonière 1968, an Alsatian, Riesling Reserve Exceptionelle Auslese 1961, to two fine, mature clarets, Château Petrus (Pomerol) 1953, and Château Magdelaine (St Emilion) 1945 en magnum, ending with the Barsac, Château Coutet 1959. It may appear odd that the red wines were all clarets at both dinners. The burgundies, of equally exalted calibre, were served at the final banquet of the Convention, which was held at the Mansion House in the City of London, by courtesy of and attended by the Lord Mayor, the delegates having returned by another special train (with champagne and lunch) in the morning. Without a doubt the Torquay part of the Convention was enjoyed most by the delegates; for years afterwards I often heard American members talk about The Imperial with the happiest of memories. The only adverse comment made by one of them was that salad was not part of every meal . . .

9
Mergers and Anniversaries

9

In the late summer of 1969 speculation was rife, and several hints and guesses were published suggesting that The Imperial was being sold. For a while the rumours were strenuously denied by the hotel and the various groups said to be the purchasers. There is no smoke without fire, however, as was proved once more when it was announced towards the end of September that the Torquay Hotel Company Ltd, owners of the Imperial ever since it was first opened in 1866, had sold out to Trust Houses, one of the large British hotel groups. This group originally started life many years ago to promote good service and value mainly in small country inns, but had been changing its image by advancing more and more into the international hotel field.

Having acquired such important properties, with great traditions, as Brown's Hotel and the Hyde Park Hotel in London, to give only a couple of examples, and a number of resort hotels in holiday areas abroad, it was logical that The Imperial, with its luxury and fine gourmet image, should be the next target on the Trust Houses' shopping list.

The management and board at Torquay had realised for some time that a change from being just one single unit would be desirable from every point of view, from purchasing to marketing. Various avenues to this effect had been explored, such as the possibilities of taking over other hotels, and it was finally decided that it would be preferable to become a part of a larger organisation. Negotiations took some weeks and the final offer made by Trust Houses amounted to £1,250,000. When the two biggest shareholders—the families of Michael Chapman and John Wollen (Chairman of the company) between them held more than 50 per cent of the total—accepted the offer, the rest was a mere formality; but in any case it was considered a fair and favourable offer and went through without hitch.

All concerned were assured that The Imperial would continue exactly as before. Trust Houses set up a new company within the Group which was to control their luxury hotels in Portugal (Dona Filipa, Vale de Lobo), Spain (Reina Cristina, Algeciras), Mallorca

(Villamil) and Barbados (Sandy Lane). The Imperial, Torquay, was to be part of this group within a group, and Michael Chapman was to run it as Managing Director. The advantages to The Imperial and Torquay in general were appreciated and welcomed, for the hotel is now 'promoted' through the Continental and overseas hotels under the same top management. The result of this has been a larger, more international clientele, a mutual benefit for all the units in the set-up. True enough, Michael Chapman could no longer give his attention exclusively to The Imperial, but its management was placed in the capable hands of the late Austin Begley, for many years the Manager.

Indeed, the change had no adverse effect on the running and prosperity of The Imperial. The Gastronomic Weekends continued as before, gaining ground all the time, and an entirely new departure was the first 'Connoisseur Weekend' held in November 1969. It was the first of four such events that winter season, organised in conjunction with the important art magazine of the same name. Its theme was 'Silver and Diamonds'; the other three dealt with 'Ceramics, Glass and Bronze', 'Paintings' and 'Eighteenth-century Furniture' respectively. In each case talks and discussions with demonstrations were given by experts of the top rank in their various fields. These weekends created considerable interest and attracted a new, different clientele, albeit they have never become quite as popular and well attended as the gastronomic ones. In subsequent seasons the magazine *Apollo* became the Imperial's partner, and eventually experience gained over a few years led to the establishment of the most successful Art and Antiques Weekends with Arthur Negus, the much loved and admired TV expert and personality.

The Gastronomic Weekend at the end of January 1970, devoted to the food and wines of a particular part of Brittany, the so-called 'pays Nantais', was unusual as not only the restaurateur, M Duteil, came over with his kitchen team, but also a sizeable delegation of leading citizens—winegrowers to a man—from the vicinity of Nantes; they were representing the ancient Ordre des Chevaliers Bretvins, one of the traditional wine fraternities of France.

I had been made a member (Chevalier) of the order some time previously, and one of the purposes of the delegation's visit was to inaugurate a British branch (bailliage). This was done in a colourful ceremony by the Grand Maitre, the Marquis de Goulaine; I was made the Baillie de la Grand Bretagne, and several friends, including Michael Chapman, were made Chevaliers of the order. The French enjoyed their visit greatly. We met at breakfast in the dining-room every morning, and an enormous amount of hand-shaking was obligatory as each of them arrived. I was highly amused one morning, when a charming and very anglophile aristocratic winegrower sitting opposite was observed to spread marmalade on the kipper he was eating with great relish. It was not long before I found the explanation for this seeming eccentricity. When a mutual friend, sitting next to him, who was a great tease, saw him attacking the kipper, he casually enquired: 'Aren't you having any marmalade?' 'Why should I?' the Comte de X asked in return. 'Well,' was the convincing reply, 'simply because no self-respecting English gentleman would think of eating kippers without marmalade!' This had the desired effect and I have been wondering for years afterwards if the Comte de X ever found out.

Meanwhile, things did not stand still in the wide world. Less than a year after The Imperial became part of Trust Houses, in May 1970, it was announced in London that there would be a merger between Forte's and Trust Houses, creating a £100,000,000 'leisure combine'. Trust Houses Forte—the name of the group was some years later changed to Trusthouse Forte—had at the time of the merger 226 hotels worldwide, besides inns, restaurants, entertainment centres, industrial catering, airport catering and even its own travel agencies. It was considered to be the biggest hotel and catering empire in Europe. Mr (as he then was) Charles Forte declared at the conclusion of the merger arrangements: 'The combination of the companies will mean that we shall have the finest management in this field certainly in Europe, and, I venture to believe, in the world.'

Michael Chapman continued as Managing Director of overseas hotels, a grouping which not unexpectedly included The Imperial, Torquay. When, towards the end of 1971, he was moved to become Managing Director of THF (Trust Houses Forte) London Hotels Division, The Imperial was moved into that division. Commenting on this transposition the *Caterer & Hotelkeeper* aptly remarked: 'It is perhaps a tribute to the unique links between the two that a Torquay hotel should be first considered overseas, then in London, at the movement of its creator. But ... the two are almost literally inseparable.'

Meanwhile Chapman continued to live at Torquay, commuting to London for the week and back to Torquay each weekend. The day-to-day management of The Imperial was still in the capable hands of his

---

(*overleaf*) The indoor swimming pool, which is part of the Relaxation Centre, opened in 1972 (*Nicholas Horne*)

long-standing and loyal right-hand man, the late Austin Begley. By now the kitchens were run by George Hamilton, who took the famous Gastronomic Weekends in his stride. In fact it was he who presented a British Week at the Grand Hotel in Rome a few months earlier and made a great success of it. On this occasion the Imperial team had splendid co-operation from BEA, who flew over the essential supplies daily—Dover soles, Devonshire cream, fresh salmon, etc. There was talk about a repeat performance in Milan the following year.

Development of the hotel has not stood still. A wide range of new amenities became available with the opening early in 1972 of yet another new extension of the building. For many years The Imperial has been a much sought-after venue for top-level business conferences and meetings, on account of its luxurious accommodation and service and the multiplicity and spaciousness of its public rooms. The advantage of the new, purpose-built Conference Centre is that it can be available at all times, regardless of the needs of other guests staying in the hotel. The new Conference Hall, named the Astra Room, is beautifully situated, overlooking the gardens sloping to the cliff-edge and Torbay. It has specially designed seating for up to 500 persons, a stage with the most up-to-date equipment for conference presentation, both audio and visual (eg overhead projection, sound system, TV, electric and gas points, spotlights, etc). There are full bar facilities, and outside a magnificent terrace overlooking the unique view. Fully airconditioned, it also makes a perfect concert hall or can be turned into a glamorous setting for a dinner-dance.

The Relaxation Centre on the floor below, which was completed at the same time, has a wealth of the finest facilities. Behind its fully glazed tall doors an attractively designed heated indoor swimming pool provides bathing in warm water all the year round. From the edge of the pool terraced steps lead to the rest of the new 'Imperial Relaxation Centre'. The lavishly designed sauna, massage and treatment rooms are staffed by a resident physical fitness consultant and qualified masseuses. It was justly claimed that the equipment and personnel available would compare favourably with the best of health clubs and 'farms'. To mention only a few, in addition to sauna and massage, there are facial toning massage, deep rejuvenating massage, underwater massage, soda foam baths, seaweed baths and herbal milk baths, ultra-violet and infra-red ray treatment, vacuum suction, passive exercise and several other beauty treatments.

Synchronised with the opening of the Conference Hall and the Health Centre another new concept was launched, the 'Slimming in

Luxury' scheme. This was an effort by The Imperial, so well known for its gastronomic achievements, to introduce an entirely new approach to keeping fit, recuperating health after illness or surgery, and weight-reducing. Special low-calorie diets are offered to augment the facilities of the Imperial Relaxation Centre. The specially devised menus, scientifically controlled by nutrition experts, clearly show the amount of calories contained in each portion of the various dishes listed. The idea is to enable guests to enjoy the luxurious setting of the hotel, participate in its social life and entertainments, and at the same time improve their health and achieve a reduction in weight; all this without the hardships and austerity usually associated with such facilities elsewhere.

Michael Parkinson, the TV personality, performed the formal opening. He recalled that it was fourteen years since he was last there. 'The hotel has changed and improved in the intervening years,' said Mr Parkinson, 'and is quite irresistible. It had the means of pleasure, and now, in its Relaxation Centre, of cure.' After an inspection tour the distinguished guests were invited to lunch. All the splendid dishes

The Relaxation Centre was formally opened by Michael Parkinson in 1972. He is seen at the head of the bath, with Michael Chapman, then Managing Director of Trust Houses Forte London Hotels, at the extreme left (*J. L. Knowles*)

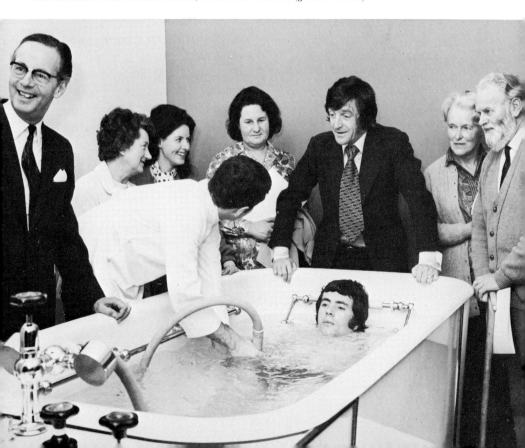

displayed on the colourful buffet table had little numbers on cards placed beside them, indicating the number of calories each portion would contain. Luckily, we were not restricted to portions on this occasion, helping ourselves to such delights as Swiss mountain beef and grapefruit segments, smoked salmon, fresh trout, roast beef, curry, baked veal escalopes and any number of salads and vegetables.

This was a most attractive demonstration of the 'Slimming in Luxury' scheme. In actual practice, the slimming guests would have to keep their total intake down to 1,500 calories per day—this would permit the odd aperitif or glass of wine—hoping to lose a good bit of weight. We were told that some early guinea pigs lost a stone in a fortnight while fully enjoying the fun of the fair.

The old-established BBC television 'Holiday' programme, presented by Cliff Michelmore, picked the Jura Weekend (January 1973), one of the by now equally old-established Gastronomic Weekends, to present to its viewers in glowing terms. When the BBC team, led by Tom Savage the producer and John Carter his reporter and commentator, arrived at the hotel in full force with their equipment of cameras, lights and the rest, there was some anxiety as to how all this would blend with the guests.

It soon became clear that Tom and his helpers would merge successfully into the crowd, and by their tact and care they rather enhanced the pleasures of the weekend. In fact, it became obvious that they enjoyed the event as much as everybody else. Shown on the screens on the following Thursday night, a full nine minutes were devoted to the Gastronomic Weekend, giving viewers a fair idea of what it was all about. John Carter's comments were most favourable: he claimed the weekend was 'not just eating and drinking, but the artistic pursuit of gastronomic experience. Of course in pursuit of that experience you could travel to the Jura itself, tucked between Burgundy and the Swiss border—indeed, for most of the guests here it would be quicker to go to France than down to the West Country. Most of those I talked to were experienced travellers and I got the impression that it was the atmosphere of The Imperial that appealed to them. A cross between travelling first class on a very steady liner and being a member of a jolly pleasant club.'

Later in the programme he said: 'The Imperial's gastronomic weekends have been imitated by many other hotels in Britain. If you want to spend your holiday money on good eating, you'll get value all right in Torquay.'

The first Art and Antiques Weekend under the auspices of Arthur

Negus, with Bernard Price as his collaborator, was an instant success (March 1973) and laid a firm foundation for similar weekends held regularly ever since; it attracted 250 guests. One of the great attractions was that they were able to bring their own treasures for the experts to assess. To quote from a current newspaper report: 'On the lap of one middle-aged lady there sat a stolid ceramic lion, name of Androcles, birthplace the Staffordshire potteries of the nineteenth century. Another "student" brought a beautiful Sevres vase, another a mahogany fiddle and yet another a lace fan.'

There was the attractive young woman who brought with her the family treasure in the shape of a miniature wooden chest with drawers, for Arthur Negus's expert identification. Family legend had it that, since her grandfather brought it back from Russia, it had been made there, before the days of Rasputin who was often a dinner companion of the charming lady's grandfather. But, as so often happens, family legend was wrong, for the little chest was identified as indisputably English-made. Nevertheless the piece must have retained its charm for the lady and her grandmother who are the only members of the family who know how to open the little drawers; a secret device works on a secret spring. There was much to be learned by all of us in the audience, such as that all eighteenth-century porcelain figures have brown eyes, or the fact that one can tell an old paperweight from a modern reproduction by the extra weight of the old one ...

'Objects of Virtue' was the title of one of the lectures given by Bernard Price, who told us that the term has been used for centuries to describe objects of great beauty and rarity, and that in the distant past these might have been thought to have magical powers. Nowadays they can include such things as miniatures painted on ivory, books with rare leather bindings, Chinese snuff bottles and carved oriental figures. We also learned that the most booming collectors' items in 1973 were those of the Art Nouveau period.

It had become the usual practice for the first Gastronomic Weekend of the season to be dedicated to the International Wine & Food Society and not to involve a visiting restaurant and its chefs. The one held in October 1973 had an interesting theme. To celebrate the Society's fortieth anniversary, each lunch and dinner was a replica of a historic menu of one of the meals served during the early months of the Society's life, as originally planned by the late founder-president André Simon. Fortunately, not only were the old menus available, but we were greatly helped by the guidance found in André's own notes and comments on the various dishes.

This was a test of skill for the hotel's young and recently appointed chef de cuisine, John Duncombe. He had the advantage of having been involved in many Imperial gastronomic weekends, for he had first joined the kitchens in 1967 (under J. Elvin) as chef de partie, then worked his way up through the kitchen hierarchy as demi-sous-chef and later (in George Hamilton's time) as premier sous chef. He acquitted himself remarkably well, his performance being critically scrutinised by the many members of the Society present. In the words of a greatly respected old member, 'The meals were a great credit to him, showing a versatility which it would be difficult to match anywhere these days.'

The same gentleman—who incidentally is one of the most faithful followers of the gastronomic weekends since their inception—made this further comment: 'It was, of course, impossible to match the food with the wines that were used forty years ago, but Messrs Averys of Bristol, probably the oldest and most reputable of the family firms left in the wine-shipping trade, had matched the menus with present-day

At a Gastronomic Weekend in January 1975 (*l to r*) John Duncombe, Head Chef of The Imperial, Michael Chapman and M Julien Nicolle, chef-patron of the H Du Guesclin, Mont-St Michel (*Eric Tall*)

equivalents and the Society's founder would certainly have approved of them ... This was a first-rate effort and a credit to all concerned, both in the production and presentation.'

By the end of 1974 events had turned full circle. Michael Chapman was promoted to the position of Chairman of the London Hotels Division, his presence in the capital then being required for only a few days every month; in addition he retained special responsibilities in connection with the Group's hotels in Portugal and Barbados, to which far-flung outposts he was expected to make one or two trips during the year. The rest of the time he was to be able to devote to the personal direction of The Imperial, once more as its Managing Director. This change pleased his many devotees among the hotel's clients, who had felt his absences during the previous five years.

He returned in time to see and personally supervise the latest addition to the hotel which was nearing completion. To the west of the Conference and Health Centre, the so called West Wing, which was once upon a time the Villa Marina, had been pulled down and on its site the Imperial Court Flats have been built. These are virtually an extension of the hotel, with the same unique situation overlooking the gardens and the vista of Torbay. All the facilities of The Imperial were made available to the inhabitants of the new flats, including the most recent additions, the Relaxation Centre, the indoor and outdoor swimming pools, tennis and squash courts, and of course the restaurant and the hotel's own entertainments and night club.

The flats were offered for permanent residence or for tenants' holidays, with luxurious fittings and equipment and all the usual hotel services—porterage, cleaning, maids and waiting staff—to complete the picture of gracious living. All have an entrance hall, living room, two bathrooms and a kitchen, with two or three bedrooms. They soon found tenants: I have got to know several of them over the last few years, and they have joined happily in the life of the hotel—their presence has added another useful dimension to the pleasant life there.

During the latter part of the 1970s there have been some particularly memorable gastronomic weekends. The one in March 1977 was notable, if only for a minor detail: it was named after a wine instead of a region or district, the Muscadet Weekend. In view of our established ties with the Bretvin Ordre, we made this a celebration of the seventh anniversay of the inauguration of the British Bailliage.

This time, in addition to representatives of the parent Ordre in Nantes, the Bailliage of Belgium also sent a delegation. The cuisine and chefs came from Le Tillac Restaurant (at the Frantel hotel in

Nantes), and as well as serving Muscadet with several of the lunches and dinners, we also managed to put on a tasting, at which eight different wines from different growers and shippers were shown. Six of these were of the 1975 vintage, one 1974 and one 1976—the last-named being of special interest, as it will be remembered that that was an exceptionally warm summer; the wine, resulting from a hot and dry harvest, differed from the usual fairly frugal young wine. It was noticeably fuller, and perhaps a little short of acidity, not at all a typical Muscadet. It goes without saying that during the same weekend we also had an impressive Bretvin ceremony—stage-managed by Michael Chapman—at which a few more worthy chevaliers were duly invested.

This was the first full year for the Imperial's new General Manager, who arrived towards the end of the previous year (December 1976). Harry Murray came straight from South Africa, where he had been heading two five-star hotels in succession in Johannesburg. Before his overseas appointments he had extensive experience in the British hotel industry, his last job before going abroad being as General Manager of the Majestic, leading hotel in Harrogate, where in fact I had met him, so he was no stranger to me. He very soon settled at The Imperial; in fact the man and the hotel must have been made for each other. He ably fulfils the role of principal host when Michael Chapman is away, at the various gastronomic and other weekends and events. He also maintains an excellent personal 'presence' towards the guests, and is often seen greeting them on arrival and going round the dining-room chatting to them at mealtimes.

1977 was Her Majesty's Silver Jubilee Year, and The Imperial joined in the celebrations of the nation by holding a special weekend early in October with 'An Exhibition of the Finest British Products & The Gastronomy of Britain'. The exhibition was presented in the spacious Astra Conference Room and consisted of purely prestige British products; exhibitors included such great names as Rolls-Royce (shown by Jack Barclay, their largest distributor, who by chance were celebrating their fiftieth anniversary), Garrard (the Crown Jewellers), Floris (perfumery, est 1730), Whitbread, Johnnie Walker Whisky, Jackson's of Piccadilly (alas, it is no more), Jaeger, the Dutton-Forshaw Group with the best BL cars, Thos Webb's Edinburgh Crystal, Asprey, several leading fashion houses, etc.

The format of the 'Best of British' Weekend apart from the special exhibition, was that of a Gastronomic Weekend—with a difference: 'The Imperial selected typical dishes from various parts of the United

Kingdom to show that British produce and cooking skills can take their rightful place in international gastronomy.' It opened with a London dinner, which included such specialities as 'London Particular' Green Pea Soup, right down to the dessert, Lemon Posset with King Harry's Shoestrings; at the reception there was Bristol sherry and the first (white) wine was Pilton Manor 1976. Saturday's lunch, preceded by Whitbread's Jubilee ale and cider, represented Wales, with Cream of Leek and Potato Soup, Saddle of Welsh Lamb, and cheese from Caerphilly—where else?

The Gala evening saw a reception with whisky-based cocktails (or champagne) and a true Scottish dinner of Smoked Salmon with Arbroath Cream Boats, Scotch Broth with Pearl Barley and Roast Highland Grouse Garnished Balmoral Style with all the trimmings ending with a dessert: Bonnie Prince Charlie Drambuie Cream Surprise.

It was appropriate that the Sunday morning wine tasting—a regular part of the programme at gastronomic weekends—should on this occasion present the 'Best of British' too. Mounted by the English Vineyards Association, it showed twelve wines, coming from vineyards in many parts of the country and demonstrating that the revival of English viticulture, started in the last 10–15 years, was well on the way. A press comment was: 'All were very worth while—certainly as worthy as many of their continental counterparts.'

Plymouth gin was the base for the cocktails preceding the West country dinner, which was based on well-liked Imperial specialities. This concluded a highly successful occasion, during which there were several non-gastronomic highlights, fashion shows, raffles and gifts— the total proceeds of which were donated to HM's Silver Jubilee appeal. The most memorable and moving part of the full programme was the impressive performance of the Band of the Royal Marines, when they beat retreat in the middle of the ballroom on the gala night.

The highest accolade to The Imperial as a conference centre came in the same year (1977), when it was chosen as the scene of the little-publicised but all the more high-powered 'Bilderberg' conference. As usual on these occasions, the delegates included some past and actual European prime ministers, international bankers, politicians and professors. In vain did reporters and photographers beleaguer the hotel's precincts; security was total, and Lord Home, who was that year's chairman of the meeting, refused adamantly even to allow a group picture of the leading delegates to be taken as a souvenir for posterity. Remarking on the strictly enforced privacy the unhappy

At a Jura Gastronomic Weekend in February 1979, Michael Chapman introduced the visiting chef, M André Jeunet, of the Hotel de Paris, Arbois and Mme Jeunet. M Jeunet's Consommé au Sauvagnin was included in the Burgundy, Lyonnais and Jura Gala Dinner during the Centenary Weekend

reporter of the *Daily Telegraph* wrote: 'Bulky-looking American Secret Servicemen joined forces with English Special Branch to patrol the maze of corridors inside the hotel, while local uniformed policemen peered under cars and poked behind bushes.'

In the kitchens he saw a chef putting the finishing touches to his contribution. He had sculptured four all-sugar globes of the world topped by white doves and olive branches. 'They are not for eating, just for decoration,' he explained. As usual, much praise was given by the delegates to the hotel and its staff for the smooth organisation of its services. The only aggrieved participant was a Scandinavian ex-prime minister, whose luggage had been flown to Tokyo instead of Torquay—such an easy mistake for an airline to make . . .

The 1978–9 season of Gastronomic Weekends was the eighteenth, and the first one in October, the first-ever Dutch Weekend, brought to the round dozen the number of countries represented. Eight weeks later (1 December 1978) came an important milestone, the hundredth Gastronomic Weekend, an occasion for a great celebration.

It was difficult to think out a programme which would successfully epitomise the ninety-nine others that had gone before. It was necessary to narrow down the field a little, and considering that the vast majority of the participants and meals and dishes in the past came from France—the French Weekends have also been the most popular with the guests—the Centenary Weekend would depend entirely on the cuisine of France.

We had a full record of every single dish served during those eighteen years, and endeavoured to present a representative selection of them during the Centenary Weekend, in such a way that each distinct gastronomic region of France would have its rightful place. Finally we managed to establish a division into five regions, one to be represented at each meal; Friday had a Bordelais, Charante, Dordogne and Basque country dinner, Saturday lunch was from the Rhone Valley and Provence, Saturday's Gala Dinner from Burgundy, the Lyonnais and Jura, Sunday lunch combined Alsace, Champagne and Paris and finally Sunday's Farewell Dinner reflected Brittany, Normandy and the Loire. The five regions—or perhaps one should say groups of regions—were marked on a map-diagram printed in the programme and each menu.

But this was not all; each dish of every meal was the speciality of a particular restaurant, as presented during their own appearance in a past weekend some time during those last eighteen years. Thus each menu showed with each dish the name of the restaurant and the chef responsible, as the following example shows:

THE BURGUNDY, LYONNAIS AND JURA GALA DINNER

* * *

Terrine maison aux foies de volailles
(Maitre Alix, Les Trois Domes, Lyon)

* * *

Consommé au Sauvagnin
(M. André Jeunet, Hotel de Paris, Arbois)

* * *

Filets de sole 'La Mère Guy'
(M. Roger Roucou, La Mère Guy, Lyon)

* * *

Filet de boeuf au Fleurie à la moelle
(Restaurant Troigros, Roanne)

* * *

Soufflé glacé Martiniquais
(M. Perronet, Chapeau Rouge, Feurs)

Discussing strategy in the kitchen for the Perigord Gastronomic Weekend in January 1980 (*l to r*) M Patrick Huillot, the visiting chef; Mme Alice Vayssouze, owner of the Hotel Palladium at Alvignac-les-Eaux and Geoffrey Woodward, second-in-command of the Imperial kitchens

Altogether nineteen dishes were served during the five meals; they were not intended to represent the best of all those years, but were suitable representative selections to make well-balanced meals. It was up to our own chef de cuisine—there were no visiting chefs this time, it would not have been practical to assemble all nineteen of them—John Duncombe, to tackle the whole lot. He took on what one writer described as the biggest challenge of his career and succeeded in a remarkable way.

Champagne in abundance, a sparkling exhibition by Asprey's, another appearance of the Royal Marines band in the ballroom, where Billy Munn's orchestra was playing—he retired in the following year—late-night revels in the newly revamped night club—now called La Pigalle (sic)—and a special celebration reunion of the Imperial Gourmet Club, all made for one of the most memorable Gastronomic

Weekends. Special prizes were offered to those who had attended longest and most weekends, and claims were received from several people and couples who had been to ninety or so of the ninety-nine weekends held in past years. Thus regular supporters were rewarded and encouraged.

The highlight of the 1979–80 season of weekends was the third in the series (30 November to 3 December 1979) which was dedicated to the person who has been responsible for developing The Imperial into one of the great hotels of the world. It was to celebrate the double anniversary of Michael Chapman, Managing Director—fifty years a hotelier and forty years at the helm of The Imperial.

Described by one writer recently as 'Hotelier Imperial', he came to re-open the hotel, as described earlier, in the first year of the last war. Since then, ably supported by his wife Tim, and with unparalleled enthusiasm and imaginative skill, he planned and carried out the complete modernisation and rejuvenation, transforming a respectable but ageing hotel into one of the finest and best equipped resort hotels in Europe, if not in the world. He also found time to give active support to the advancement of the hotel industry as a whole. Over the period of his wider responsibilities in having overall charge of the Trusthouse Forte Group's overseas hotels and later its London luxury hotels, he steadily continued his full involvement in the running of his first love, The Imperial.

The response from all his friends and long-standing hotel clients to this very special Gastronomic Weekend was overwhelming, and several months before the event not only was all the accommodation at the hotel fully booked, but there appeared to be a serious problem of over-booking. Old friends had to be asked to accept being 'farmed out' in nearby hotels, so as to be able to take part in the festivities.

The programme was carefully planned in an endeavour to surpass everything that had gone before. As many readers will remember, the meals were replicas of others served on important landmark occasions during those forty years of Chapman rule at The Imperial: The Victory celebration dinner (as served on VJ night in 1945), a Game Lunch, as served to the International Wine & Food Society Convention in 1969, the Centenary Gastronomic Weekend Dinner (from the celebrations a year before), a Grand Buffet Lunch as served during the Olympic Yachting Regatta in 1948, and finally a repeat of The Imperial's Centenary Gala Dinner presented in 1966.

There was an exhibition of Rolls-Royce cars through the past five decades and the latest models, put on by Wadham Stringer, the RR agents for Devon, in the Astra Room and a display of exquisite porcelain, china, glass, objets d'art and precious gifts by Coleridge of Highgate in the Gold Room. Fashions through the 'last half century' were presented by Gabe of London in a lively show in the ballroom on the Friday after dinner. Music for dancing was provided by the Imperial Quintet with Jacqui Clarke (Billy Munn had retired after an almost uninterrupted thirty years at The Imperial) and afterwards in the Pigalle night club downstairs.

A memorable highlight of the weekend came when, on the first evening during the champagne reception, a resumé of Michael Chapman's whole career was presented on the lines of the well-known 'This is Your Life' television programme. The interviewer was Mrs Nicky Knapman, Michael's daughter, who followed his life story step by step, bringing in a number of other characters as the story progressed. It was an endearing and charming performance, towards the end of which the 'subject' was joined on the platform by a number of long-serving members of the staff: Jim Mason (back of house supervisor), 40 years; Dennis Eldergill (bars manager), 37 years; John Barratt (night-club manager), 37 years; William Brown (carpenter), 30 years; Joseph Brzozka (head waiter), 27 years; Helmut Erdpresser (ballroom head waiter), 24 years; Alex de Paulis (head waiter), 24 years; R. Camm (maintenance manager), 20 years; John Horwell (head barman), 20 years; Mrs G. Stafford (chambermaid), 20 years; R. Kendrick (chef de partie), 20 years.

On the Saturday night the pressure on space was so great that the Haldon Room had to be used as an extension of the dining-room, and later dancing in the ballroom was stopped to allow the Royal Marines Band to march in and give another of its superb performances.

The usual Sunday morning reunion of the Imperial Gourmet Club had to be held in the ballroom on account of the exceptionally large number of members present. Since the formation of the club, Michael and I had been joint secretaries; feeling it was time for a change, after a few suitable words I proposed that Michael be elected chairman and that Harry Murray take his place as joint secretary. Needless to say, the proposal was carried unanimously. This reunion was also made unusual and memorable by the presence of a salamanazar of Bollinger (contents the equivalent of 12 bottles), which had been sent to Michael Chapman as a tribute by the head of the champagne house. A glass or less was poured for all present to drink the health . . . There were many delightful touches—displayed on the buffet table at Sunday's lunch was a portrait in pastillage of Michael Chapman—an excellent

The reunion of The Imperial Gourmet Club during the Special Weekend celebrating Michael Chapman's double Anniversary (2 December 1979). Michael Chapman (*centre*) was assisted in the opening of the celebratory Bollinger salamanazar by Stephen Pinchbeck (Deputy General Manager) while the author, as Joint Secretary of the Club announced Michael Chapman's election as Chairman (*Eric Tall*)

likeness, and it turned out that the 'artist' was not one of the chef-patissiers from the kitchens, but a young floor-waiter, Trevor Bailey, who enjoys decorative sugar work as a hobby.

The concluding dinner on Sunday night—preceded by plenty of Krug, Grande Cuvée—with a certain amount of formality proved worthy of the celebration. The Loyal Toast was proposed by the Mayor of Torbay, Councillor L. S. W. Howard, JP and the one and only other toast was to 'The Imperial, Torquay and its Managing Director', proposed by Sir Frederic Bennett, Member of Parliament for Torquay; Michael Chapman in his response expressed his thanks and appreciation with suitable modesty.

The greatest fun of the evening—if not of the whole weekend—was yet to come. The printed programme for the weekend simply stated 'Music through the Half-century', and in keeping with this a small

137

platform had been erected in the middle of the dining room, from which the entertainment was to come. During coffee and liqueurs, all the guests were given what looked like song-sheets, which bore this title: 'Michael Chapman says "THANK YOU FOR THE MUSIC"'. On the face of it, the programme was simply intended to create nostalgic pleasure, listing the songs popular through the five decades, beginning at the 'turn of the twenties' with 'Tea for Two', going on with the thirties, forties, and so on. The performance was given by a small group of professional actor-singers, who earned a lot of applause as the programme progressed. We were so absorbed in watching and listening to the performance that the disappearance of Michael Chapman from the table went unnoticed—until he appeared again, costumed and made-up on the platform, having joined the others in one after another of their songs with tremendous elan and professionalism. Then it dawned on the audience who it was that took the part of such great characters as Charlie Chaplin, Bud Flanagan and a succession of others, singing their appropriate songs with the rest

Michael Chapman performing as Charlie Chaplin during the after-dinner entertainment on the Sunday night of his double Anniversary Weekend, 2 December 1979 (*Eric Tall*)

During the Breton Gastronomic Weekend of 22–5 February 1980, the Balliage de la Grande Bretagne of the Ordre des Chevaliers Bretvins celebrated its tenth anniversary with due pomp and ceremony. Here the author, the Bailli (*right*) greets Michael Chapman on joining the Council as its newly appointed 'Seneschal'

of the group. His unexpected, unheralded and extremely 'professional' performance made a tremendous impression on all those in the vast dining-room, and the applause after the finale, 'The singing seventies: Thank you for the Music', brought the house down.

The performance brought back happy memories to those among the guests who were old enough to recall the merry Christmases spent at The Imperial up to more than ten years ago. For the star performer of this evening was the same man who entertained them so magnificently year after year by glittering and hilarious pantomimes, ballets and revues put on by the staff of The Imperial for Christmas. Not only was Michael Chapman responsible—with Mrs Phil Kitley-Carter, the one-time hostess—for producing these shows, he also invariably took a leading part, be it that of principal boy or girl, or prima ballerina. At other times he would sing a duet with Billy Munn—leader of the Imperial orchestra from 1947 until 1978—playing the parts of two chambermaids, Russian spies, or a couple of poodles, lampooning the guests and the 'goings on' at the hotel.

10
How It Works Today

10

Philip wears a splendid top hat and a smart dark green uniform with shining brass buttons; he is the doorman at The Imperial and his friendly, welcoming smile is the first human contact for the arriving visitor, regardless of whether he is an old 'regular' or coming for the first time. In the former case, the feeling is unmistakeably that of arriving home after a short or long absence: 'It is so nice to see you again!'

Once you have been greeted and helped out of your car or taxi, everything will be done for you; from now on, you should not have a care in the world—the cosseting has commenced. Your luggage is being taken care of and so is your car, which will be parked carefully in the hotel's spacious garage.

Having been directed to the reception desk and given your name to the charming receptionist, the only formality is the 'signing in'. After this you will be conducted by another of the receptionists to your suite or room. There, even if you have seen it many times before, you will still enjoy that unique view outside and the ample, contented feeling you get as you look around inside. Now you cannot fail to notice the flowers for your wife with a card on which the General Manager personally greets her. Incidentally, he may have done so in person as you came to reception on your arrival; Harry Murray does this whenever his work allows it, as Michael Chapman did before him, over many years.

A knock on your door signals the presence of your own valet with your luggage, only minutes after arrival. He will be doing a great deal for you during your stay: collect and clean shoes left outside your door overnight (this service is fast disappearing in most parts of the world, and newcomers have often expressed pleasant surprise), 'sponge and press' your travel-weary best suit or dinner jacket. You don't even have to ask, he will suggest it himself.

After the journey, on a lovely early afternoon, with the sun shining brightly, it would be easy to decide that a refreshing swim is indicated. Depending on the time of year, there is a choice of two pools, one outdoors, splendid and mosaic-lined, with heated seawater, and the other indoors, also heated, but with fresh water, enjoyable in all weathers. With the appetite refreshed and a little sharpened, afternoon tea suggests itself. It could be ordered to be brought to one's room, of course, but it may be more interesting to see a bit of life and go to the long gallery lounge, where tinkling piano music comes from the adjoining ballroom. The tall, elegant headwaiter—Helmuth Erdpresser, with The Imperial for more than a quarter-century—greets you with a smile and shows you to a table. Do you like Indian or China tea, milk or lemon?

A trolley is wheeled up by a young waiter or waitress, with a wide choice of 'dainty' sandwiches (cucumber, tomato, egg, sardine, etc), buttered malt bread and a delicious-looking assortment of cakes and pastries, all there for the asking. Tea arrives, and it will be noticed that China tea is served in a china pot, Indian in the usual silver plate. A pleasant interlude this, taking in the old-world charm of the setting and observing one's fellow guests. If afternoon tea could be made as enjoyable in other places as it is here, it would not be such a disappearing custom.

The evening paper must have arrived by now, and you find it at the hall porters' desk, near the main entrance. Here you will probably meet Ray Wilson, the head porter. Like his well known and liked predecessors—Arthur Sangster and Gerald Taylor—the first was also known for being the father of a famous tennis player, who now runs an excellent sports shop in the town, and the second as a top breeder of dachshunds in his spare time—he is in charge of all the valets and page boys, as well as the other hall porters. His department is there to make life easy for the guests, to arrange for their every need and whim. Not only will they call you in the morning, get your daily and Sunday papers, order taxis, look up trains and aeroplanes, make bookings for travel or theatres, arrange for flowers to be sent, find you if you are wanted on the telephone (should you not be in your room at the time), send clotted cream to your friends, get you a horse to ride, but they will also advise on the more unusual problems that may arise.

Back to your room in time for the BBC news—yes, of course there is colour television in every room, as well as radio and a direct-dialling telephone with a special signal indicating that a message is awaiting at the switchboard. Relax, have a bath if you like, and change; soon it is time for the first aperitif of the evening . . .

Dennis Eldergill is in supreme charge of the bars, and most evenings he will be found in person behind the bar in the Eugenie

Room or the Regency Lounge. He has been not very far off forty years at The Imperial, and more than twenty in his present job. Not only is he a great expert on drinks in general, but a virtuoso of cocktails; a full-page photograph of him appeared in John Doxat's book dedicated to the Dry Martini, *Stirred—Not Shaken*. Here is a quote from the Book: 'Serving as he does an elite clientele, he goes for ultra-dry Martinis—about 99 per cent gin or vodka—but even then he can't satisfy everyone. Knowing one woman to like her mix as dry as possible, he decided to serve it without any vermouth at all—what is known as a Naked Martini. Perhaps predictably, back came the complaint, "not dry enough".'

'One must remember personal quirks,' says Dennis, 'In the old days, for Eugene Higgins, the American millionaire, I had to add a dash of Angostura, Prince Bertil of Sweden liked a dash of Pernod in his Martinis.'

'Dennis is seemingly ambidextrous: his right hand mixes the Martini, while simultaneously his left rotates ice in the glasses to chill them.'

John Horwell, head barman, is Dennis's deputy, and takes charge in his absence; they are assisted by an excellent, well-trained team of young men and girls, who take the drinks to your table if you are sitting down. The busiest times in the bars are before lunch and dinner; the service is, as one would expect, quick and cheerful.

The thinning-out of guests in the bar—and the sharpening edge of the appetite—suggest that it must be time for dinner. Entering the dining-room you will be greeted by a distinguished-looking black-suited personage, coming towards you from his desk by the entrance. Should he not have met you before, on mentioning your name, he will lead you with a welcoming smile to your table. This is Ron Greaves, restaurant manager for the last fifteen years or more. He is the personification of the ideal maitre d'hotel, of fine appearance, dignified and elegant manner, and having a keen sense of humour allied to tact and infinite courtesy. The attributes are not altogether different to those associated with diplomats, or even elder statesmen. Guests he has to look after come from all parts of the world, and he needs these skills as, in the words of a recent article about him, 'the lamb cannot be asked to sit at the next table to the lion'.

There is something commendably old-fashioned about the way in which Ron Greaves does his work. He learned his trade when restaurant staff were strictly trained and he is determined that his staff should maintain the highest degree of courtesy and efficiency. Should you ever blunder into the restaurant say half an hour before the first guests arrive, you will see him giving instructions to all the staff, including a careful explanation of the dishes on the menu, their composition and the way they should be served.

Another writer has summed it up neatly: 'Rest assured that if you drop a fork or just a hint, make a sign or heave a sigh, Mr Greaves will take your point—and all will be well.' And the same goes, almost equally, for the head waiters, both meritorious veterans in the service of The Imperial: Joseph Brzozka and Alex de Paulis, one of whom will look after you from now on, throughout dinner supervising the service by the station waiter and commis, plus the wine waiter.

Your table is allocated to you, usually for the length of your stay, and during that time the same members of staff will be looking after you. The most desirable tables here are those nearest to the vast windows overlooking the sea—the view of what has been called 'the English Bay of Naples'—but the back half of the restaurant is raised, so that there is a sea-view from almost everywhere.

You will be presented with the menu for the set dinner (or lunch) of the day, and also the extensive à la carte menu, with a large number of classics and Imperial specialities. On the set menu are listed four or five dishes for each course, and for the end of the meal there is the usual ample cheese board and a 'sweet trolley'.

Having settled what to eat, the wine waiter appears, offering the extensive Imperial wine list. Your order for wine is taken to another important personality who is based in the so-called 'dispense', where your bottle will be made ready for service. This is Morris Smith, MS (the initials stand for Master Sommelier, a title not easily awarded to the best men in the profession). He is highly skilled and knowledgeable on every aspect of the subject of wine, as I know for I often converse with him on the subject, one dear to us both. You can be sure that your bottle will arrive in the right condition and at the right temperature.

During dinner you will enjoy the beautiful setting, the alert and efficient service and the attractive way in which each of the dishes you have ordered is presented for aesthetic and appetising effect—this is a great forte of the Imperial kitchens, inspired by John Duncombe, the versatile chef des cuisines.

(*opposite*) Part of the cold buffet in The Imperial's dining room (*The British Tourist Authority*)

In the euphoria resulting from a good dinner you agree to the suggestion to move for coffee and liqueurs to the ballroom or the lounge next door. Here the head waiter, Helmut, will greet you as an old friend, having already looked after you at tea time, and show you to a table, neither too near nor too far from the band, which is playing up-to-date but not 'pop' music for dancing. George Ramsay, the hotel's host, will probably come and make himself known to you—he is responsible for making people feel at home and relaxed, helps with arranging bridge fours, and of course dances with ladies, especially those without a partner. He is a superb dancer himself and is available during the day for dancing lessons. A pleasant way of spending an evening, whether one is a keen dancer or just likes to watch others while listening to the music, especially the singing of the good looking blonde soloist.

If you think it is too early for retiring when the band stops playing in the ballroom, it is time to adjourn to the night club, the Pigalle, where John Barratt, another old Imperial hand, and his colourfully dressed staff will take care of your needs for liquid refreshment until the early hours (1 am or later).

'And so to bed'—the chambermaid has done her work, curtains drawn, fresh towels in the bathroom and beds turned down and prepared. On your pillows will be found the order forms for breakfast, should you wish to have it in your room. All you have to do is to fill in the time it is to be served, mark the items of your choice and hang it outside on the door-handle, not forgetting also to put out shoes for cleaning . . .

In some ways perhaps breakfast is the most important meal in a large luxury hotel such as The Imperial. This is the conclusion reached by David St John Thomas, who was allowed behind the scenes at the hotel while researching for his *Breakfast Book* (published by David & Charles). There is of course the choice for every guest between having breakfast served in the bedroom or suite and getting dressed to have it in the restaurant. In favour of the second choice is the fact that one can decide at the last minute what to eat: the full selection of traditional British breakfast dishes, or just a 'Continental', abbreviated form. On the morning of his visit, Mr Thomas reports, he found that about one-third of the guests chose the restaurant, the rest preferred the informality of their rooms.

In the restaurant, with—if you are lucky—the sun streaming in and the blue waters shimmering outside the windows, you will be cosseted by Mr Greaves and his team, and can order almost anything you can think of. No one would bat an eyelid if you were to ask for caviar followed by rump steak. A friend of mine felt like a fresh grilled herring on the first morning after his arrival to find that, unfortunately there wasn't one to be had. 'I am terribly sorry sir,' said his waiter, 'but I shall make sure you have herring tomorrow.' And sure enough his fish was served—not one but two perfect specimens. Another friend asked for a particular, lesser-known brand of marmalade—it was produced without trouble.

It will be no problem deciding what to do after breakfast and during the rest of the day. The two swimming pools have been mentioned already, two hard tennis courts, squash courts (a 'pro' is available), miniature golf, and four different golf courses within easy reach. Every kind of water sport is available and can be arranged for guests: sailing, fishing, or water-skiing, and riding can be booked at nearby stables. Sauna, massage, electrical and other beauty treatments in the Imperial Health Centre, hairdressing for both sexes, are all there for the asking. For the ladies especially there are ample shopping opportunities inside the hotel from the various showcases: cosmetics, jewellery, chocolates, clothes, accessories, objets d'art, books and periodicals and every kind of gift. Within a short walk, Torquay has a number of excellent shops.

Venturing a little further, the best beauty spots of the Devon countryside are within easy reach. The hall porters are well informed and always willing to help with advice and making arrangements.

The experience of staying in The Imperial makes it clear that the guests' impression of perfect ease and carefree comfort is not brought about simply by the built-in furniture, equipment and technical devices. The human element makes a unique contribution to the achievement of the friendly, welcoming and helpful atmosphere which pervades every aspect of life there. The resulting feeling of being cosseted is largely due to the ingrained attitude of every member of the staff; all give you the impression that their sole purpose in life is to make the guests happy. There is nothing servile in this, it is simply an understanding of how their job should be done to the best effect. It makes The Imperial one of the world's great hotels, for it is an attitude not always found elsewhere.

How does this come about? It is clearly the product of a combination of training, discipline and a tradition of exemplary leadership. We have no clear record of the quality of guest-staff relations going back before the last war, but it is safe to assume that they must have been similar to those of today, as this was always one of the top hotels, right from the beginning. In any case it must have been easier to achieve superb staff co-operation in Victorian and even Edwardian times.

We have a clearer picture of how it has been done since 1939 when Michael Chapman first took the helm. It will be remembered that he took charge of an empty shell, and the staff had to be reassembled and augmented, in fact one could say that he had to start from scratch. He has told me more than once that he firmly believes that the staff are one of a hotel's greatest assets. Without a doubt this has been the guiding principle of his management. Right from the beginning, during the difficult war years, he never lost sight of it. Having arrived on the scene, one of his first actions was to turn the disused space which had been the garage for the by then defunct hotel bus into a staff club, which was to be run autonomously by a committee elected by the staff. The hotel provides the premises and other fixed outgoings (light, heat, etc), and bar profits are divided among the members, partly on the basis of what each of them spent in the bar. I have been privileged to be invited once or twice for a drink by kind staff members, and found the experience most enjoyable. On enquiry I find that not many hotels provide this facility for their staff.

Loyalty is bred from such gestures, but this is only one of the facets of good and effective handling of staff. Chapman has always endeavoured to maintain as permanent a brigade as possible; this is borne out by the numerous long-serving employees mentioned in other parts of this book. At the same time, he has always been respected by his staff as a strict disciplinarian; he has practised the discipline relentlessly but without any bitterness or malice, like a benevolent dictator; in fact I heard it rumoured that at one time they called him 'father' below stairs. He certainly manages to imbue the people working in the hotel with the need to please the clients all the time, right from the beginning of their training, and this teaching is passed on by the heads of departments.

Mrs Phil Kitley-Carter, the much-loved hostess employed at The Imperial for a number of years, put this in a nutshell during an interview with a magazine, way back in 1968, and it could not be better expressed today; it also throws some light on the back-room work, which has not changed: 'The success of this hotel is due to the friendliness of the staff. And it comes from the top; I mean Mr. Chapman himself. Guests are welcomed by every department. When people come back we always try to give them the same table and remember their names. Of course it's quite impossible to remember everybody: how many people do you think come here in one year? So we all have a guest list, and when we see HA beside the name we know that means 'Here Again'. If I don't recognise the face I say something like: "I hope you have got a nice room this time, which is it?" Then I look up the room number on the list and get the name that way. It's true that Mr. Chapman sets a high standard of courtesy and good humour; he bustles past, always busy, always pleasant, smiling at some guests, talking to others, kissing the hands of another few . . .'

Harry Murray, the General Manager since 1976, finds it easy to follow in the same tradition. (Michael Chapman, Managing Director, nowadays keeps to the background a little.) He is a smart, athletic type, and few people realise that every morning, before starting work at 8am, he goes for a good, long jog in all weathers. Next he goes round the dining room, talking to the guests at breakfast, before returning to his office to deal with the day's correspondence.

Around mid-morning he calls the daily conference with all the heads of departments. With his deputy, Stephen Pinchbeck (who is also responsible for 'Food & Beverage'), the managers of the house and of personnel respectively, the head housekeeper, head chef, head porter, restaurant manager, bars manager, head of reception, maintenance manager, occasionally the chief accountant, and if need be the Managing Director, all attend to discuss progress and problems of the day and also forthcoming events. This is also the time when special weekends, Gastronomic, Gardening (Percy Thrower), Art and Antiques (Arthur Negus), etc, and the special needs for the various conferences, meetings and banquets, are discussed. These daily discussions form important direct links in the chain of command between top management and all the staff, whose members keep up the close contact with the hotel guests while performing their multifarious duties . . . always with a smile.

Appendices

BOARD OF DIRECTORS OF THE
TORQUAY HOTEL COMPANY LIMITED 1969
(At the time of the takeover by Trust Houses Ltd)

C. J. H. Wollen (Chairman)
Appointed Secretary 1926; elected a Director 1936; elected Chairman 1947.
His father C. S. Wollen, had been Chairman since 1910, having joined the
Board in 1903. Solicitor; former Commodore of Royal Torbay Yacht Club.

H. L. Goodson (Vice Chairman)
Elected a Director 1941, following his father, Sir Alfred Goodson, who had
been a Director since 1935. Past Commodore of Royal Dart Yacht Club;
Chairman, Sail Training Association.

H. M. Chapman (Managing Director)
Appointed Manager 1939; Managing Director since 1944.

Sir Peter W. Hoare
Elected a Director 1958; Senior Partner in C. Hoare & Co, Bankers.
T. L. Mooyart
Elected a Director 1958; Chartered Accountant.
Mrs H. M. Chapman
Elected a Director 1964 and appointed Assistant Managing Director.

CHAIRMEN
OF THE TORQUAY HOTEL COMPANY LIMITED

Sir Lawrence Palk, Bart, MP (later Lord Haldon)	1863–83
Col John Campbell	1883–5
W. F. Splatt	1886–93
Col the Hon Edward A. Palk	1895–1910
Cecil S. Wollen	1910–47
C. John H. Wollen	1947–69

MANAGERS OF THE IMPERIAL

Thomas Webb	1866–78	
George Hussey	1878–95	
F. Fischer	1895–1904	
J. Worster	1904–10	
C. W. Hore	1910–39	(Managing Director from 1935)
H. M. Chapman	1939–	(Managing Director from 1944)
A. J. Begley	1965–1976	(General Manager from 1969)
Harry Murray	1976–	(General Manager)

Bibliography

Mary C. Borer, *The British Hotel Through the Ages* (1972)
A. C. Ellis, *An Historical Survey of Torquay* (1930)
S. P. B. Mais, *Glorious Devon* (1934)
C. Matthew, *A Different World* (1976)
Percy Russell, *A History of Torquay* (1960)
D. Taylor, *Golden Age of British Hotels* (1977)
J. T. White, *A History of Torquay* (1878)
Caterer & Hotelkeeper, Centenary issue (1978)
John Doxat, *Stirred—Not Shaken: The Dry Martini* (1976)
Torquay Directory; *Torquay Times*; *Herald Express*; and a large number of
newspapers and periodicals, too numerous to list individually

Index

(Page numbers in italics indicate illustrations)